# AGE OF THE MAHABHARATA WAR

# AGE OF THE MAHABHARATA WAR

KOTA VENKATACHELAM

GYAN

*Published by*

Gyan Publishing House
5, Ansari Road
Daryaganj, New Delhi-110002
Phone: 011-47034999, 9811692060
E-mail: books@gyanbooks.com

*Distribution Network*
gyanbooks.com
India, USA, Canada, UK, Australia



ISBN: 978-93-7316-663-6 (PB)

First Published, 1913

2nd Impression 2025

*Printed at:* Gyan Press, Delhi.



**AGE OF THE MAHABHARATA WAR**

Arthur: KOTA VENKATACHELAM

# AGE OF THE
# MAHABHARATA
# WAR

AUTHOR
"Bharata Charitra Bhaskara"
PANDIT KOTA VENKATACHELAM

Arya Vijnana Grandhamala- Publication - 25

# AGE OF THE
# MAHABHARATA
# WAR

AUTHOR

"Bharata Charitra Bhaskara"

PANDIT **KOTA VENKATACHELAM**

---

For Copies :

Dr. K. N. SASTRY

Ananda Ayurvedic Drug Research Institute & Pharmacy

**ADRIPS**

Kotavari Buildings, Besant Road,

Gandhinagar, VIJAYAWADA - 520 003.

(SOUTH INDIA)

"BHARATA CHARITRA BHASKARA"
"VIMARSAKAGRESARA"

**PANDIT KOTA VENKATACHELAM**

Author

# PUBLISHER'S NOTE

After forty years of Research in the field of Indian History, the Author PANDIT KOTA VENKATACHELAM has ransacked the indigenous literature dealing with our Indian History as also the great bulk of the Eastern and Western books, the writings of the Western Indologists and their Indian followers and has refuted the illogical arguments of the Western Historians, established the truth of the historical data detailed in our Puranas from the Mahabharata War 3138 B. C.

The Author already published 24 books and this "AGE OF THE MAHABHARATA WAR" is the twenty fifth in his series.

Pandit Kota Venkatachelam is our father and is now known, after assuming the ochre robes in the year 1957 as "Jagadguru, Sankaracharya" SRI ADWAYANANDA SANKARABHARATI SWAMY, (Peethadhipati of Sri Abhinava Virupaksha Peetham). The Author commenced the writing of this book "Age of the Mahabharata War" in the year 1957 and completed it in the year 1959, and after few days of the completion of this book he attained Siddhi on 12-11-1959 A. D., or Kali Saka 5060, Vikari, Kartika Suddha Trayodasi.

Since a long time this book is in dark and now it is seeing light with the co-operation given by our Near and Dear.

*KOTA SRI KRISHNANANDAM*
*Dr. KOTA NITYANANDA SASTRY*
Publishers.

# AGE OF THE MAHABHARATA WAR

## CONTENTS

# THE AGE OF THE MAHABHARATA WAR

## PREFACE

श्लो ॥ व्यवसायात्मिकाबुद्धि रेकेह कुरुनंदन ।
बहुशाखाह्यनंताश्च बुद्धयोऽव्यवसायिनाम् ॥

भगवद्गीता २-४१

"The cultivated mind is one-pointed and its determinations are firm.

The uncultivated mind is a prey to fancy and its decisions are fickle and fleeting."

(Geeta-2-41)

The conclusions arrived at by cultivated minds, matured by the study of the traditional lore, stand firm and unambiguous. The opinions of uncultivated minds, ignorant of the traditional lore vary from time to time and lead to controversies. The truth of the sentiment is illustrated in the writings of the modern historians of India, who, without any attempt to acquaint themselves with the ancient literature of the land, and with implicit unquestoning faith in the veracity or validity of the writings of the foreign historians who had deliberately concocted a false history of our country with a view to minimise the antiquity of our civilisation, deprive us of self-respect, and keep on for ever in bondage and under their domination, endeavour unsuccessfully to reconstruct a cogent and comprehensive history of the country and present a pathetic and deplorable spectable to all genuine lovers of the land. Unless and until our historians ignore completely efface from their minds for a time, the false historical writings of the foreigners which closed their vision and blind them to the truth and sit at the feet of the indigenous scholars of the traditional lore of the land or study the Epics and the puranas and other historical writings in our ancient literature, they will never be able to learn or determine the true history of our country.

A true historical determination should stand the test of time and never be liable to change from time to time. It cannot be decided by majority opinions. It cannot be the result of conjectures and theories or ingenious arguments and counter arguments. It must be based on the evidence of eye- witnesses, or records based upon the reports of eye- witnesses.

The sage Vyasa, revered in the country as a very incarnation of God has recorded in the Mahabharatha, our sacred national epic, that 36 years after the termination of the Great War in which the Kauravas were all defeated and destroyed and the Pandavas came out victorious. Sri Krishna, who played a promminent part in the War and in securing the vicotry for the Pandavas, stuffled off his mortal coil and from that year the Kaliyuga commenced. Vyasa was a contemporary and an eye- witness of the battle. The facts of the Great War and the parties to it and the result of it are admitted by one and all ancient native writers and modern foreign and native historians. But the date of the War so specifically mentioned by Vyasa is ignored and varied and fanciful determinations of the same are suggested by these historians. Where is the need for conjectures and theories in the matter and how can conjectures and theories lead us to the truth?

Sri Vyasa was present on the scene at the time of the war and during the period of the negotiations and the attempts to avert the war that just preceded it and himself played a prominent part in the deliberations and negotiations and advised the wicked sons of Dhritarashtra, who were responsible for the war. They did not heed his advice but persisted in their attitude which brought about the war and perished in it. He was actually present at the time, the common progenitor of the Kauravas as well as Pandavas, witnessed the battle in person, and recorded the story of the war with the title "MAHABHARATA". Therein the time of the war is thus specifically narrated.

The Kauravas were all destroyed in the war. The Pandavas were victorious. The eldest of them Yudhishtira was crowned Emperor of Bharat on the 10th day after the completion of the battle. In the 36th year of his reign, Sri Krishna, the incarnation of God, who has played a prominent part in the war and contributed considerably to the success of Yudhishtira ceased his mortal existerce and returned to Vaikuntha. On receipt of this news the monarch placed his grandson 'Parikshit' on the throne and proceeded on a pilgrimage tour to all the chief shrines in the country accompanied by his consort Draupadi and all his four brothers. The Kaliyuga is reckoned from the moment of Sri Krishna's niryana.

This is what we find in the Mahabharata. This account is well-known to all the people of Bharat the laymen as well as the scholars, with the least acquaintance with our epics and puranas. It was prescribed in the calendars of the country that since the close of the Dwapara Yuga and the commencement of Kali, all the people of Bharat should, in the pres.

cribed narration of time and place in connection with their normal daily ritual, thenceforth substitute, Kali Yuge, Pradhama Pade (the first quarter of Kali) for Dwapara Yuge, Thuriyapade (the fourth quarter of Dwapara). On the first day in the month of Chaitra in the year Pramadhi, which was a Friday at 2-27'-30" the advent of Kali was celebrated in this country with the performance of the prescribed rituals, gifts and sacrifices. It was a sacred day, the first day of a Yuga, (ie. Yugaadi) for them since the Kali era commenced, upto the present in 1959, 5,060 years have passed. And the Western historians themselves have recognised the commencement of the Kali Era as at 2-27'-30" hours on the 20th of February in B. C. 3102 in their Christian Era. This has been accepted without any question by all the European Historians of our country from Sir William Jones who laid the foundations in 1774 A. D for the prevailing modern history of Ancient India down to Vinicent Smith who wrote in 1915. 36 years before it i.e., in 3138 B. C should be accpted naturally as the time of the Mahabharata war. While the evidence is so unambiguously available in our Mahabharata which we hold as sacred as the Vedas, to ignore it and to suggest various dates based on various conjectures and theories for the date of the Mahabharata war is preposterous. The 'Sage Vyasa' has recorded in the Mahabharata itself that he began the composition of the poem in the year 1 of Kali and completed it in 3 years. When the War described by him is accepted as historical, why should the date of it mentioned in it be discarded? If they had recognised the date of the Mahabharata war as 36 years before Kali, as it is mentioned in the poem and calculated the times of the reigns of the kings of the several dynasties that ruled over the different kingdoms in the country according to the Matsya, the Vayu and the Brahmanda, the Vishnu and the Bhagavata puranas, the true history of ancient India could have been ascertained long ago and established. But the puranas and other historical writings of the country have been discarded as un-reliable and inscriptions, coins, buildings, the accounts of foreign visitors have been accepted and declared as more reliable and really authentic sources for our history, even after a century of laborious researches, we have not been able to fix the date of the Mahabharata war, the corner stone of Ancient Indian history on the basis of any clear and cogent evidence. Without any such waste of time and energy and money, etc., with an elementary equipment for historical study could have discovered it in an hour from the Mahabharata and the Puranas.

The foreign historians were interested in reducing the antiquity of the literature and civilisation of Bharat and for that purpose to push up the time of the Mahabharata War as far as possible, towards modern times. Hence they did not tackle the problem so far; and now that the false history of ancient Bharat, concocted by them has been established in the country and firmly rooted in the minds of the students who have been taught the same in schools and colleges; now the question of the date of the Mahabharata war is taken up and attempts are being made to fix it some-where between 1500 B. C. to 900 B. C. If it is a genuine attempt to ascertain the truth, how is it there is no invitation to the scholars in the traditional lore of the country, to produce if they can, any reliable and verifiable evidence in their possession concerning the matter. It is a problem which can be solved, if even by reference to the indigenous literature of the country in Sanskrit and never by the Western historians or their Indian disciples, with their utter ignorance of all knowledge of Sanskrit. How is it no notice is taken of publications in which it is openly declared that the history of Ancient India taught in our schools and colleges, is false and concocted. How is it the challenge is not accepted, the conclusions disputed or the arguments refuted? How is it the authors of such publications are not consulted in the present endeavour to ascertain the date of the Mahabharata war?

When the recorded histories of Magadha, Kashmir and Nepal and the epics and puranas of the land, all declare the time of the Mahabharata War unequivocally and unanimously, where is the need for searching for other evidence for it. Why this pathetic clinging to the false determinations of the Western, European scholars?

The propaganda carried on by the European historical scholars among the students in our colleges is clearly exposed by Maha-mahopadhyaya Dr. Haraprasada Sastry, M. A., Phd., who writes from experiencne.

"In the eighties, my European friends advised me not to touch the Ramayana, the Mahabharata and the Puranas for the purpose of getting Indian history from them. They worked hard with coins, inscriptions, notices of foreign travellers, archaeology, sculpture, architecture, for extracting chronology and history from them. In fact they studied every thing but the puranas. But ho! Mr. Pargiter and Mr. Jayaswal now produce a chronology from the puranas themselves which agrees in outline with the one prepared with so much toil of nearly 150 years by the orientalists. (Vide, J. B. O. R. S. Vol XIV P. P. 325, 326). But our Indian historians have not paid any heed to the advice and regrets expressed so eloquently by him. They continue to cling to the ways and methods of the European historians. They have not ventured to discard them and to attempt to construct the history of their own country based on a study of the national literature in the epics and puranas. The minds of those destined to err cannot be brought back to the right path. We may have to wait further for auspicious times for the true history of Bharat.

According to the evidence available in our epics and puranas, the date of the Mahabharata war is 36 years before Kali. Now, ie., by A. D. 1959, we are in the 5060th year of Kali. So reckoning on the Christian era, the date of the Mahabharata war works out to 5096-1958 (elapsed year) = 3138 B. C. This is the correct determination inwhich there can be no change. But some of the modern scholars are of opinion that it may be fixed at 1500 B. C. or some other date. 'May be also' means may not be and we argue, should not be. Such opinions are mere conjectures and can never amount to determinations. That alone is truth which does not vary from time to time or from place to place, accor. ding to our traditional intellectual standards.

By the Sruti we hear : "Thrikala badhyam Satyam, Badhyam Midhya" ("त्रिकालाबाध्यं सत्यं, बाध्यं मिथ्य"). That which remains unchanged through the past, the present and the future, that alone is the truth. That which changes is only an illusion i. e., that which appears to be till it is enquired into and disappears on investigation of its nature. Modern history, i. e., the ancient history of India of our modern historians is all such an illusion, a false structure which cannot stand critical scrutiny. Rao Bahadur P. V. Kane, who presided over the Indian History congress at Waltair in 1953 went wrong in interpreting the 3 rd verse in the 13 th chapter of the Brihat-samhita and arrived at the date 2448 B. C., for the time of the Mahabharata War. The author (of this book) had even then exposed the mistake in the interpretation of the verse in his publication "Indian Eras". For a detailed criticism of the interpretation of the verse, reference may be made to the VI chapter in this volume.

There can be no other true history of the Mahabharata war than the "Mahabharata" and the puranas by Vyasa who had witnessed the war and recorded the events as he witnessed them in his immortal writings. The evidence to the contrary advanced by the Western scholars is all hearsay evidence. It cannot be acceptable to true historians. Messrs. V. B. Athorvel (Kirlaskar Wadi, Satara District), Dr. Kali Nath Nag, Taraknath Bhattacharya have fixed the date of the Mahabharata war at B. C. 3102 and Dr. Fleet at B. C. 3146, M. Troyer, Dr. Kuppayya, T. S. Narayana Sastry, B. A. B. L., M. Krishnamachary, A. Somayajulu, Nadimpalli Jagannadharao, Rallabhandi Subbarao, M. A., B. Ed., C. P. Vaidya and many others have proved with irrefutable arguments and proofs that it is B. C. 3138. In the determinations at B. C. 3102 and 3146, there is a little discrepancy from the truth but as the discrepancy is so slight, we extend our congratulations to the sponsors of the dates also for approaching the truth.

Ever since the Western historians, with the deliberate intention to reduce the antiquity of the civilisation and culture of Bharat, began their attempts to bring down the time of the Mahabharata war nearer to modern times, and along with it as a consequence the times of the literary works and the greater personalities of ancient Bharat and advanced the fantastic theories that the 'Mahabharata' was a composition of the 8th century A. D., and the Rigveda of a thousand years earlier, and published them about the middle of the 19th century, keen resentment had been felt and spirited protests uttered by pathetic Indian scholars. This dispute thus started a century ago.

The late Justice Triambakatelong, who is noted for his sobreity and open-mindedness in Indological research, writes:-

"It appears to me, I confess, that it is these 'likings' and 'satisfactions' and 'forgone conclusions' lying in the back of most of the logical artillery which the European scholars have brought to bear upon the chronology of our ancient literature, it is this that is temporarily doing damage to its antiquity. Not only hypothesis have been formed on the weakest possible collection of facts, but upon such hypothesis further superstructures of speculation are raised. And when this is done, the essential weakness of the base is effectually kept out of view."

But the Western scholars enjoyed the advantage of the prestige of the ruling race and the patronage of the government. They could therefore brush aside the protests of the Indian scholars and to incorporate their fanciful theories and fantastic arguments into the textbooks prescribed for schools and colleges in the country, upon which the Indian youth were brought up and to treat with indifference and even derision the historians (and their writings) who attempted to construct the true history of the country on the basis of the ancient literature and historical writings. Truth will be ascertained only after a dispassionate study of the two sides to any controversy. The desire to study the arguments of the other party, to meet the arguments and discuss the validity of the arguments on either side and to arrive at the truth is conspicuous by its absence among our modern historical scholars. They cling to their false histories and refuse to take the risk of exposing them to criticism and discussion.

There are three historical sources for determining the true and correct time of the Mahabharata war indisputably. The first of them is the history of Magadha. It is available in our Puranas. This is now usually considered the history of Bharat. In this we find the lists of the kings and ruling dynasties of the kingdom of Magadha in unbroken sequence beginning with 36 years before Kali i. e., B. C. 3138. The lists are found in the writings (the Puranas) of Sri Vyasa himself who was an eyewitness to the Mahabharata war.

The second is the history of Kashmir. This gives us the lists of kings that ruled over Kashmir beginnig with about 300 years before the Mahabharata war which it fixes at 36 years before kali or 3138 B.C. The accounts of the reigns of the different kings and dynasties in their histories by contemporary scholars have been strung together in this history. Attempts to construct a continuous history on their basis had been made in the past by as many as twelve authors. Some of these compositions incorporate traditional information and hearsay reports here and there with the original accounts by contemporaries. Therefore, there are variations and conflicting accounts in some parts among their twelve histories. So, Kalhana a scholar of comparatively recent times, collated them, compared them with one another and with inscriptions of the kings and other historical material available to him, eschewed the doubtful and conflicting portions and evolved a cogent, consistent and continuous history of Kashmir. But the modern scholars have attributed to him wilful changes and exaggerations and additions to the lists of kings, their time and the times of their reigns and edited them in their own way and out of all recognition with the original.

The third source is the history of Nepal which begins 1000 years before the Mahabharata war and gives us lists of the kings and their reigns with dates on the Kali Era. All the three sources have been tampered with freely, edited and misinterpreted by modern historians to suit their prejudices and to corroborate their theories of the reduced antiquity of the Mahabharata war. It is the books written by such Western scholars and their disciples that are studied in our schools and colleges. Hence the true history of Bharat has not been available to our youth. The basis of such a true and correct history of Bharat is the time of the Mahabharata war. It is essential to ascertain and place beyond doubt this corner stone of the chronology of ancient Indian history. Hence, an attempt is made in this volume under different Topics, to fix the time of the Mahabharata war in 36 years before Kali or 3138 years before Christ, and to establish beyond any doubt the correctness and the determination on the basis of all the evidence available in our epics and puranas, indigenous historical records and writings, astronomical treatises and inscriptions etc.

VIJAYAWADA
6-11-1959

AUTHOR.

# THE AGE OF THE MAHABHARATA WAR

## TOPIC - I

### INTERNAL EVIDENCE

### The events that led to the war

A Great Prince by name Santana, belonging to the Lunar race of Kshatriyas was ruling at Hastinapura during the period of transition from the Dwapara to the Kali Yuga about 300 years before Kali i. e., 3401 B. C. He had two sons, Bhishma by his first wife 'Ganga' and Vichitra Virya, by his second wife 'Satyavathi'. The devoted son Bhishma, renounced his right to the succession to the throne, desisted from marriage and remained a life long bachelor, to please his father. His step-brother Vichitra Viraya, who therefore succeeded Santana to the throne, in his turn begot two sons. The elder of the two, Dhritarashtra was born blind, and therefore disqualified to succeed to the throne according to law. So the right to the throne devolved on his younger brother Pandu. But out of his regard and consideration for his elder brother, Pandu placed him on the throne nominally and carried on the administration on his behalf. A princess by name Gandhari (daughter of the king of Gandhara), choose to marry the blind King Dhritarashtra. She was such a devoted and exemplary wife that she lived blind-folded to the end of her life to avoid for herself the privilege of sight, denied to her husband. She had a hundred sons by Dhritarashtra. They are the well-known one hundred Kauravas of the Maha-Bharata. The prince Pandu begot five sons, Yudhishtira and his illustrious brothers, the Pandavas. While the Pandavas were still in their boyhood, Pandu retired to the forest for austerities and passed away there. Bhishma sent for the Pandavas and arranged for the coronation of the five Pandavas along with the hundred Kauravas at Hastinapura. The malicious Kauravas tried a number of ways to bring the Pandavas to harm but failed in all their attempts. At last on the advice of 'Veda Vyasa' divided his kingdom into two parts, handed over one half, that of his deceased brother to the Pandavas, and kept the other half for himself, to be administered by his eldest son, Duryodhana whom he nominated the crown prince. Yudhishtira, the eldest of the Pandava princes ruled over the half of the kingdom that fell to his share with Indra-Prastha (or Sakra-Prastha) as his capital.

His reign at Indra-Prastha commenced in the 75 th year before Kali (i.e., B. C. 3177). In that year the Saptarshi Mandala the constellation of the Great Bear crossed over into the region of the star Magha. It remains in the Magha for a hundred years from 3177 B. C. before crossing over into the region of the next star on the Zodiac. Up till now Hastinapura was the capital of a kingdom only. The land of the Kurus was just one of the many separate kingdoms of Bharat. But the Pandavas conquered with the might of their arms a number of other kingdoms, added considerably to their inherited territory and ruled over a vast empire extending over the entire Bharat and even beyond the river Sindhu on the west and the Himalayas on the north, including the frontier Kingdoms of Yona, Hara, Huna, Romaka, Bahlika (Bactria), Darada, Turushkasthan (Turkistan), Sakasthan (East Persia) and other territories occupied by the Mlechcha (ex-communicated Hindu Kshatriyas) princes and included in the frontiers of ancient Bharat. The eldest Pandava prince, Yudhishtira thus became the Emperor of the entire Bharat, performing the Rajasuya Sacrifice, the traditional test of suzerainty.

Duryodhana, their cousin of Hastinapura was filled with envy at the glory earned by the Pandavas, invited Yudhishtira to a game of dice, and with the help of his uncle Sakuni, who was an adept at the game, defeated him in the game. According to the rules of the game, and the specified stakes for which the game was played, were obliged to spend a period of 12 years, along with their wife, the illustrious Droupadi, in the forest and another year after that, somewhere in disguise without being detected and if they happened to be detected before the year was completed, again a period of 12 years in the forest and so on, their empire to be returned to them when the term of exile was successfully completed. Thus for a time Duryodhana became the emperor by virtue of his success in the game of dice, to which he managed to entice Yudhishtira, and by no act of valour or conquest on his part. But when the Pandavas fulfilled the conditions laid down, completed the term of 12 years of exile in the forest, and 1 year of exile in cognito, and claimed their empire, he refused to return it to them. This was the reason for the Great war.

On account of the consideration that Bhishma had been a honoured prince at the Kaurava court from the beginning, ever since the times of Santana and Pandu, he participated in the war on the side of the Kauravas. He was aged 236 years at the time of the war and he was elder to VedaVyasa by about 20 years. Yudhishtira was 91, Bhima 90, Arjuna 89, and the twins Nakula and Sahadeva 88. Sri Krishna was of the same age as Bhima, i.e., 90 years. The Kauravas and all their supporters were destroyed in the Great war. All the five Pandavas won the victory and survived. 36 years after the Bharata war, the entire Yadava race, to which Sri Krishna belonged, fell a prey to internecine quarrels and perished fighting with one another at the Prabhasa Tirtha. Sri Krishna survived the Mahabharata war for 36 years, i.e., lived up to the age of 90 + 36 = 126 years and in his 126th year shuffled off his carnal body. It is so recorded in the 'Mahabharata' by 'Sri Veda Vyasa'.

The battle at Kurukshetra was confined to 18 days only. On the 19th day all the ladies of the royal family of the Kauravas proceeded to the battle field along with Kunti, the mother of the Pandavas, and Gandhari, the mother of Kauravas, for a last sight of the corpses of their husbands, sons and other relations. Gandhari was overwhelmed with grief for the loss of all her sons and in a fit of uncontrollable anger into which her grief threw her, cursed Sri Krishna in the following terms in the 25th chapter dealing with Gandhari's curse in Stri Parva of the "Mahabharata" in the verses 43, 44, 45 and 46.

श्लो ॥ यस्मात्परस्परंघ्नंतो ज्ञातयः कुरुपांडवाः ।
उपेक्षितास्ते गोविंद तस्मात् ज्ञातीन् वधिष्यसि ॥ (25-43)

" त्वमप्युपस्थिते वर्षे षट्त्रिंशे मधुसूदन ।
हतज्ञातिर्हतामात्यो हतपुत्रोवनेचरः ॥ (25-44)

" कुत्सितेनाप्युपायेन निधनं समवाप्स्यसि ।
तवाप्येवं हतसुता निहत ज्ञातिबांधवाः ॥ (25-45)

" स्त्रियःपरितपिष्यंति यथैव भरतस्त्रियः ॥ (25-46)

Gist of the curse :

'Oh ! Madhusudana, you have looked on unperturbed while Pandavas and Kauravas who were cousins, fought among themselves and perished. So you will also be a destroyer of (your) cousins. In the 36 th year to come after witnessing, helplessly the destruction of all your sons, nobles and cousins, you will be obliged to wander in the forest and be yourself destroyed in an ignoble manner. The Yadava ladies shall grieve as the Bharata ladies are now grieving'.

Such were the words of the curse pronounced by the lady in her grief and indignation at the sight of the corpses of all her near and dear on the battlefield. 36 years after the day (the 19 th day after the commencement of the Mahabharata war) according to the curse, the Niryana, demise, of Sri Krishna was predicted to occur. Accordingly it happened. In the 36 th year after the Mahabharata war the Yadava race perished and Sri Krishna passed away and from the moment of the

Niryana of Sri Krishna the advent of Kali Yuga is recognised and the years on the Kali era are reckoned and now in April 1959 of the Christian era, (the first day of the first half of Chaitra in the year Vikari) we have completed 5060 years on the Kali Era and entered on the 5061st year. 36 years before the commencement of Kali, standing in grief on the battle field, in the midst of the corpses of her children the noble lady Gandhari pronounced the curse on Sri Krishna. So it is now 5060 + 36 = 5096 years since the Great War took place. The War occurred in (5096—1958 A. D = 3138 B. C.) It is now recognised on all hands, all over the world that the Kali Era commenced at 2-27'-30" hours on the 20th day of February in 3102 B. C. The Kali Era commenced with the Niryana of Sri Krishna. So it is clear the Great War which occured 36 years before the demise of Sri Krishna, i. e., 36 years before Kali should be dated 3138 B. C. This is the correct determination on the internal evidence available in the Mahabharata itself, directly in the story of the War.

Further other confirmatory evidence available in the Mahabharata in several other parts for instance in the 1st chapter of the Mausala parva, verses 1, 7, 8, 9 and 13 say :-

श्लो ॥ षट्त्रिंशे त्वथ संप्राप्ते वर्षे कौरवनंदनः ।
दवर्श विपरीतानि निमित्तानि युधिष्ठिरः ॥ (मौसल 1-1)

" कस्यांचिद्वथ कालस्य कुरुराजो युधिष्ठिरः ।
शुश्रावव ष्णिचक्रस्य मौसले कदनंकृतम् ॥ (1-7)

श्लो ॥ विमुक्तं वासुदेवंच श्रुत्वारामंच पांडव: ।
समानीयाद्ब्रवीद्भ्रातॄन् किंकरिष्यामइत्युत ॥ (1–8)

" परस्परंसमासाद्य ब्रह्मदंडबलात्कृतान् ।
वृष्णींविनष्ठांस्ते श्रुत्वा व्यथितापांडवाभवन् ॥ (1–9)

**वैशंपायन उवाच :–** Vyasampayana says :—

श्लो ॥ षट्त्रिंशेथततोवर्षे वृष्णीनामनयोमहान् ।
अन्योन्यं मुसलैस्तेतु निजघ्नु: कालचोदिता: ॥ (1–13)

Gist of the verses :

'As the 36th year after the war and the curse of Gandhari approached, Yudhishtira observed many evil omens. At the same time he came to know of the annihilation of the entire Yadava race due to internecine quarrel, and mutual slaughter on account of the strange "Musalam" which resulted from the curse of the sages whom they happened to insult. On hearing the news of the death of Balarama and likewise of Sri Krishna, Yudhishtira summoned all his brothers and conveyed the sad news to them and they all tried to console one another for the calamity. Thus the narrator Vysampayana narrated the story to King Janamejaya that "in the 36th year after the Mahabharata War the warriors of the Yadava, Vrishni, Bhoja and Andhaka races all perished in the mutual slaughter occasioned by the fatal 'Musalam'

Again in the 2nd chapter of Mousala Parva we find in the verses 18 to 24 :—

श्लो ॥ एवंपश्यन् हृषीकेश स्संप्राप्तं कालपर्ययम् ।
त्रयोदश्या ममावास्यां तां दृष्ट्वा प्राब्रवीदिदं ॥ (2-18)

" चतुर्दशी पंचदशी कृतेयं राहुणा पुनः ।
प्राप्तेवै भारतेयुद्धे प्राप्ताचाद्यक्षयायनः ॥ (2-19)

" विमृशन्नेवकालं तं परिचिंत्य जनार्दनः ।
मेने प्राप्तं सषट्त्रिंशं वर्षंवै केशिसूदनः ॥ (2-20)

" पुत्रशोकाभिसंतप्ता गांधारी हतबांधवाः ।
यदनुव्याजहारार्ता तदिदं समुपागमत् ॥ (2-21)

" इदंच तदनुप्राप्त मब्रवीद्यद्युधिष्ठिरः ।
पुराव्यूढेष्वनीकेषु दृष्ट्वोत्पातान् सुदारुणान् ॥ (2-22)

" इत्युक्त्वा वासुदेवस्तु चिकीर्षुः सत्यमेवतत् ।
आज्ञापयामास तदातीर्थयात्रा मरिंदमः ॥ (2-23)

" आघोषयन्त पुरुषां स्तत्र केशवशासनात् ।
तीर्थयात्रासमुद्रेवः कार्ये ते पुरुषर्षभाः ॥ (2-24)

Gist of the verses:

Sri Krishna noted the ominous circumstances of the solar eclipse on 13th day of the second fortnight of the month, the 14th day having lapsed and the 13th and 15th occurring together on the same day, just as it happened on the occasion of the Mahabharata war, and reflected "the same omens were observed at the time of the Mahabharata war, in which the entire race of Bharata perished, perhaps the Yadava race will perish now". And he recollected the curse of Gandhari and further reflected. "It is now 36 years since the Mahabharata war. Perhaps the prediction in her curse is coming true. The omens observed at the time of the war according to the report of Yudhishtira are all to be observed now. Let the Yadavas perish at a sacred place". He resolved, and arranged for the movement of all the males of the Yadava and allied tribes to the Prabhasa Tirtha for the 'Suryoparaga Snana (bath)'.

Again in the Maha Prasthanika Parva we find in the description of the action taken by the Pandavas on receipt of the news of the distruction of the Yadavas etc., Vysampayana says in verses 2, 6 to 9 of chapter I.

श्लो ॥ श्रुत्वैवंकौरवोराजा वृष्णीनां कदनंमहत् ।
प्रस्थानेमतिमाधाय वाक्यमर्जुन मब्रवीत् ॥ (1-2)

" ततोयुयुत्सुमानाय प्रव्रजन् धर्मकाम्यया ।
राज्यंपरिददौ सर्ववैश्यापुत्रे युधिष्ठिरः ॥ (1-6)

" अभिषिच्य स्वराज्येच राजानंच परिक्षितम् ।
दुःखार्तश्चाब्रवीद्राजा सुभद्रां पांडवाग्रजः ॥ (1-7)

" एषपुत्रस्यतेपुत्रः कुरुराजो भविष्यति ।
यदूनां परिशेषश्च वज्रोराजा कृतश्चयः ॥ (1-8)

" परीक्षिद्धास्तिनपुरे शक्रप्रस्थेच यादवः ।
वज्रोराजा त्वयारक्ष्योमाचाधर्म्ये मनःकृथा ॥ (1-9)

Gist of the verses :

'On receipt of the news of the destruction of the Yadava, Vrishni and Andhaka etc., tribes, Yudhishtira resolved to renounce the world and go on pilgrimage and addressing Arjuna, said "I have resolved to renounce the world and go on pilgrimage. So send for Yuyuthsu the son of Dhritarashtra by his Vysya wife and entrust the administration of the empire to him and instal Parikshit as the king of the Kurus. Then he turned to the grief stricken wife of Arjuna, 'Subhadra' and said 'the son of your son 'Parikshit' will be the king of the Kurus, your nepew 'Vajra,' the son of Aniruddha the son of Sri Krishna i. e., Sri Krishna's grandson, will be the king of the surviving Yadavas. Parikshit will rule at Hastinapura. The Yadavas will stay at Indra-Prastha. Vajra will be their king. You will have to look after him. You should not think of accoampanying us." Just at the moment Sahadeva approached smiling and said in the verses 19 to 27 of the 1st chapter of the Mahaprasthanika Parva "Mischievous practices and quarrels are arising among men due to their avarice, in sales and purchases, and encroachments on the neighbourer's lands. Injustice has set in. 'Kali seems to be at work'.

---

Yudhishtira heard the words and felt disgusted with life and said "we have lived long enough. We should not stay here any longer," and removed all the costly jewels and clothes on his body, and changed into homespun and the brothers and Droupadi followed his example. They were all ready to start on the great pilgrimage, the final journey, with the sacred fire in their hands. They presented exactly same picture as when they had formerly started for the exile of 12 years in the forest. The women of the palace were all filled with grief at the sight. But the brothers and Droupadi were rejoicing, for their part. The five Pandavas, Droupadi, their consort, and a dog accompanying them, all started from Hastinapura.

The same account of the destruction of the Yadavas and the advent of Kali, with 36th year after the Mahabharata War in the Mahabharatam in the Telugu rendering by the three great Andhra poets and in the Devi Bhagavatha, 2nd Skandha, page 60 of the rendering in Telugu by Vidwan Saripella Viswanadha Sastry, M. A.

In the face of such clear, unambiguous and unanimous evidence everywhere in the ancient literature of Bharata which proves that the Mahabharata War occurred in the 36th year before Kali (3102 B. C) i.e. 3138 B. C,. and that Sri Krishna passed away in 3102 B.C and Yudhishtira and his brothers in 3077 B.C, to ignore them all, and to conjecture that the war might have occurred 1600 years after Kali, is sacrilegious.

* * * *

# THE AGE OF THE MAHABHARATA WAR

## TOPIC - II

### INTERPOLATIONS IN KALHANA'S RAJATARANGINI

Once it is accepted that the Kali era commenced, with the moment of the demise of Sri Krishna in B. C. 3102, it is obviously unwise and impertinent to attempt to locate the date of the Mahabharata War somewhere some centuries after the begining of the Kali era. It has necessarily to be attributed to a mischievous intention to deceive the Hindus and put them on the wrong track. To participate in the war at the time thus fixed for it by the modern scholars according to their misleading history, it should be necessary for Sri Krishna to come down once again from his permanent abode in heaven. Is it not surprising that the Indian historical scholars of modern times also should join in the endeavour to search for a date for the Mahabharata War some time later in the Kali era, after it is accepted by one and all that the commencement of the Kali era and the event chiefly responsible for it and synchronising with it, the demise of Sri Krishna who played a prominent part in the war, was in 3102 B. C? How is it, it dose not strike them as an unwise and useless endeavour. This thoughtless imitation of the westren historians is only a proof of their blind allegiance ingrained in them to their western masters, and utter lacking respect for the native historical literature of the country.

But one apparently formidable objection may be raised to the point of view adumbrated in these pages by a reference to verse 51 of chapter I of Kalhana's Rajatharangini, the source of Kashmir history where it is recorded that the Pandavas and Kauravas were alive in Kali 653. Here is the answer to the objection for which the earnest attention and dispassionate consideration of the reader is invited. The verse in question could not have been Kalhana's. It must have been due to interpolation or tampering with the text. It is further our contention that not only this verse I–51 but the verses I—49, 50, 54 are all due to such interpolation. They are directly contrary to the trend of Kalhana's views. Dr. Buhler procured a manuscript copy of Kalhana's Rajatharangini in Kashmir and took it over to England for getting it printed. The interpolations were most probably effected at the time, while the manuscript was being printed in England. Kalhana says in the verses I—55, 56 of his Rajatharangini that the constellation of the Great Bear moves in the region of each star for a hundred years, accepting the authority of the views of Vriddha Garga and Varaha Mihira for their calculations of the movement of the Great Bear, and declares that during the reign of Yudhishtira the constellation was in Magha. Yudhishtira's reign extended from 75 Years before Kali i. e. 3177 B. C., to 3077 B. C. This will be established with proofs and detailed explanations in the pages to come in chapter VI of this volume in connection with the discussion of

'Aasan Maghaasu Munayaha' "आसन् माघासु मुनयः" I-56 of Rajatharangini and XIII-3 of Brihat Samhita to which reference may be made. How could the same Kalhana in the same treatise declare Yudhishtira to be reigning in 3177 B. C. in one verse 56, and in Kali 653 or 2448 B. C. in another verse 51, two contradictory statements in the same breath? If we concede him capable of such self-contradiction and inconsistency, his treatise should not be accepted as a reliable source of history. He has employed as the basis for his work the era known variously as the Laukikabda, Yudhishtira Kala, the Saptarshi mana, the Kashmirabda, which began in Kali 26, or B. C. 3076. If the Kauravas and the Pandavas had been alive in Kali 653 or B. C. 2448, how could he base his history on the secular era commencing in B. C. 3076 with the ascent to heaven of Yudhishtira?

According to the account in Kalhana's Rajatharangini Gonanda-I, king of Kashmir joined with Jarasandha in his invasion of Madhura, long before the Mahabharata war, and was killed in the battle by Balarama. His son Damodara-I attempted to disturb the Swayamvara function of a princess of Gandhara and was destroyed in that connection, by Sri Krishna himself. His son Gonanda-II became the king of Kashmir in 3140 B. C. while he was yet a boy in 3138, B. C., in the Mahabharata war. All the tributary princes in the country ranged themselves on one or other of the two sides in the war. But, says Kalhana as Gonanda-II of Kashmir was a minor in his teens, his participation in the war was not solicited by either of the two parties to it, the Kauravas and the Pandavas. In proof of his statement we may also note that nowhere in the account of the Mahabharata war in the 'Mahabharata' is there any mention of an army of Kashmir. The Pandavas accompanied by their consort Draupadi commenced their ascent to heaven (Swargarohana) in Kali 25 or B.C. 3077. At that time, in memory of the great emperor Yudhishtira, in Kali 26 or B. C. 3076, on the first day in the fist half of Chaitram, when the constellation of the Great Bear crossed over from the region of the Magha to that of the next star on the Zodiac, a new era was founded called the Saptarshimana (era), the Yudhishtira Kala, Laukikabda or the Kashmirabda. So the theory that Yudhishtira and his brothers who passed away in B. C. 3076 lived later than in Kali 1600 (or 15 th century B. C.) and made war on the Kauravas is a fantastic theory. According to our Puranas and Mahabharata Sahadeva, son of Jarasandha, King of Magadha, was killed in the Mahabharata war in B. C. 3138 and then his son Somadhi was crowned king of Magadha at Girivraja the capital of the state. Somadhi was the king of Magadha and contemporary of Yudhishtira at Hastinaapura till the end of Dwapara. He survived Yudhishtira and Dwapara and continued to reign in Magadha for 22 years in Kali as the contemporary of Parikshit at Histinapura. He ruled on the whole for 58 years. Sri Pargitar has adopted the same account in his 'Dynasties of the Kali Age'. Hence, it is quite clear the Mahabharata war occurred in 3138 B. C. towards the close of Dwapara, 36 years before the beginning of Kali. When it is accepted that the Kali Yuga began on the demise of Sri

Krishna in 3102 B. C. and even the western historical scholars do not dispute this, it is ipso facto, accepted that the Mahabharata war in which Sri Krishna played the most prominent part occurred 36 years before his demise i. e., in 3138 B. C. They stand committed to the determination and they are aware of it. But, inspired by the unholy intention to reduce the antiquity of the ancient history of Bharat, they do not admit it. And to induce and encourage our Indian historical scholars to search for the date of the Mahabharata war in the later centuries of Kali, they have interpolated I-51 of the Rajatharangini into the manuscript copy at the time it was being printed in London and on the strength of it, initiated the mischievous theory. The Indian historians, their disciples, have not been able to see through this mischief and are deceived. Hence, the date of the Mahabharata war has become a tough problem for them. If only a ray of the truth should penetrate their innocent mind, it will be quite clear to them that the Great war took place in 36 years before Kali or 3138 B. C.

* * * *

# THE AGE OF THE MAHABHARATA WAR

## TOPIC - III

### THE YUDHISHTIRA SAKA

For a valid reconstruction of the history of ancient Bharat or for the correct determination of the times of the several great personalities of ancient Bharat, it is quite necessary to fix the date of the commencement of the era known as the Yudhishtira saka. After the Mahabharata battle (which was waged for 18 days) came to a close, on the 28th day after the commencement of the battle. Yudhishtira was crowned as sole Emperor of Bharat. From that time onwards the times of events have been recorded on the "Yudhishtira Rajya Kala", the new era named after the great Emperor and commencing with the date of his Coronation as the undisputed sole Emperor of Bharat, after the close of the Great War. In later times the same era has been sometimes called 'Yudhishtira saka". So the Yudhishtira Saka or periods of time measured on the Yudhishtira saka (Era) are almost the same (except for the difference of 28 days) as the periods are reckoned from the time of the Mahabharata War. So to fix the Yudhishtira Saka the time of the Mahabharata war has to be ascertained and established firmly, in the first place.

Among the inscriptions of ancient times so far discovered in India, and publishod, about 99% belong to the Centuries of the Christian Era (after Christ), and very few perhaps only one are two have been discovered relating to kings after the Mahabharata war, upto the Christian era. There is scope for apprehensions, in the circumstances that inscriptions relating to very ancient times round about the time of the Mahabharata war might have been discovered actually, but suppressed or destroyed out of a deliberate intention on the part af those concerned, to prevent the discovery of the true antiquity of the history of Bharat; and strong rumours to that effect do prevail in the nationalist circles in the country. It is, on the face of it, absurd and impossible to believe that none of the ancient kings of Bharat down to the time of the Mahabharata war i. e., 3138 B. C. had thought of leaving even a single inscription behind recording their achievements or gifts, while the numerous inscriptions discovered of the later times, after the Christian era themselves reveal a common tradition and custom of recording gifts and achievements even of the merchants and the common people in inscriptions in all parts of the country. There can be no doubt that they had to their credit many such inscriptions and many such had been discovered in the archaeological excavations carried out in the country in modern times. But they must have been, all of them, deliberately destroyed. Actually there is proof of such a destruction of one inscription in the case of the Kumbhalagarh inscription (V. S 1517) found recently in five broken pieces in several places, which, put together are found to form one inscription. It must have been discovered entire, some time earlier, broken and the pieces deliberately scattered in several places to prevent rediscovery.

vide Article. "the fragmentary second slab of the Kumbhalagarh inscription V. S. 1517 by Dr. G. N. Sarma, in the volume entitled proceedings of the fourteenth session, Jaipur; Indian History Congress, 1951".

Dr. G. N. Sarma thus comments on the inscription:

"The inscription under review, belonging to the Mamadeva's temple of Kumbhalagarh, (this temple was built by Rana Kumbha in V. S. 1517 or Saka 1382, A D. 1460) is in a form of a very small piece preserved in the Victoria Hall Museum, Udaipur. It's present form does not help us to deduce with accuracy as to why was the slab broken and who broke it? However I have been able to discover the entire text of this missed slab through the help of manuscript entitled "PRASASTHI SANGRAHA' of Saraswati Bhavan Library, Udaipur (For Prasasti Sangraha, see proceedings of the Indian Historical Records, Commission, Udaipur Session 1944, G. N. Sarma, a note on 'Prasasti Sangrha' pp. 73, 74). It consists of the transcripts of those inscriptions of Rana Kumbha (V. S. 1490-1525/1433-1468 A. D.) which originally belonged to the temple of Mamadeva at Kumbhalagarah and the Kirthistambha (the tower of fame) at Chitor".

The transcription of the second slab of Kumbhalagarh............ informs us that Bappa, a Brahmin of Anandapur (now called Arnoda), well versed, in learning, left his home with his trusty followers and came to 'Nagda' in the wild tract of Newar. He served

'Harit' who being pleased with him conferred upon him the dignity of a ruler. Here the qualifying phrase "Vipra Kshipratara Prabodha Madhuranamdaika-nishtah" " विप्रक्षिप्रतरप्रबोध मधुरानंदैकनिष्ठः " introduces Bappa in a manner which affords no ground for doubting in Bappa's origin as a Brahmin. This phrase explains the reason why all the writers have used 'Vipra' specifically for Bappa to show his origin i. e., from Brahmin dynasty. But in some of the epigraphs Bappa or his successors have been referred to as Kshatriyas, it is that Kshatriyaship which he had acquired through Harita's favour. This is why for Bharatribhatta the successor of Bappa, the Chatsu inscription (Epigraphic Indica Vol. XII, P. 13) of the tenth century A. D. used the word 'Brahma Kshatri'.... a Brahmin admitted to the orders of Kshatriya. In epic times the function of a Brahmin was of both learning and war 'Chaapena Sr. ayenavaa' "चापेन श्रायेनवा". Hence the word (Dvija) according to Sanskrit etymology, may mean Kshatriya, or 'Vipra' may mean one who sows virtue, though it usually means a Brahmin and is generally used as such. History of later early age and early mediaeval times is full of examples of many ruling Kshatriya dynasties which trace their origin from Brahmins. Thus Bappa's Brahmanic origin is in accord with the traditions of our country".

"The Fact that Bappa's Brahmanic origin was so commonly believed that even Kumbha in his commentary of 'Gita Govinda' has not hesitated to call Bappa Brahmin. Right from 7th Century A. D. to our own days" Bappa Brahmanic origin has been a popular fact. Somali inscription of

646 A. D., Aitpur inscription of 977 A. D., Chatsu inscription of tenth Century A. D., Rasiyaki chhatri inscription of V. S. 1331, Rayamal Inscription of V. S. 1545 and many others have repeatedly declared Guhilots as of Brahmin origin. The same fact has also been mentioned by mediaeval writers like Nensi and Ranchoda Bhatta.........Such attempts of suppressing the true facts suggest that the destruction of the second slab was also a deliberate action of some body who did not like to see such records exist."

## Comment

The Rajput princes known as Ranas were all Brahmins by ancestry. Their founder Bapparana from whom all the Ranas derive their descent was a Brahmin and his ancestry is all recorded in this inscription. The European historions of ancient Bharat built up fantastic and baseless theory that the Ranas were all born of the foreign races of invaders, the Sakas, Pallavas, Hunas, to the low caste native women and that these warriors of low and mixed origin were accorded the status of Kshatriyas and flattered as Brahma-Kshatriyas by the Brahmins. These theories were incorporated in the histories compiled by them and distilled into the minds of our youths for whom they were prescribed as text-books in schools and colleges. The inscription under reference contained evidence to the contrary, directly disproving their theories and upholding the traditional view of the Ranas and Brahma-Kshatriyas or Brahmins who had adopted the Kahatriya mode of life. So this inscription must have been deliberately shattered to pieces and thrown away as soon as it was discovered at first and it was the separate pieces that were later on discovered by chance due to the misfortune of the perpetrators of this act of vandalism, and put together and brought to light.

It is very likely that a similar fate had befallen other inscriptions relating to the very ancient times round about the Mahabharata War of 3138 B. C., and after 3138 B. C., to the beginning of the Christian Era.

Within a month of the close of the Mahabharata War and the coronation of Yudhishtira as Emperor of Bharat, Parikshit was born. In the 36 th year afterwards Sri Krishna passed away and from the moment of demise 2 hrs- 27'-30" on the 20th of February in B. C. 3102 the Kaliyuga commenced and events are reckoned on the Kali Era. Now 5060 years of the Kaliyuga are over and we are in the 5061st year. It is so recorded in our Annual Panchangas, native Calenders in use in the different parts all over the country. So 5060 + 36 or 5096 years is the period that has elapsed since the year in which the Mahabharata War took place, Parikshit was born, and the Yudhishtira Era was founded. So the date of the commencement of the Yudhishtira Era or of the Mahabharata War works out indisputably to 5096 - 1958 = 3138 B. C.

* * * *

# AGE OF THE MAHABHARATA WAR

## TOPIC - IV

### CONJUNCTION OF SEVEN PLANETS AND PANCHANGAS (ANNUAL CALENDARS)

Yudhishtira became the Emperor of Bharat after his victory in the Mahabharata War. In the 36 th year of his rule as Emperor, his cousin Sri Krishna who had been his strong support played a prominent part in the conduct of the war, passed away in Dwaraka. The Puranas and the Mahabharata are all unanimous in declaring that the commencement of the Kali Yuga is reckoned from the moment of the demise of Sri Krishna (ie., 3102 B. C.)

The Vishnupurana in sloka 12-2-33 says :-

श्लो ॥ यस्मिन् कृष्णोदिवोयात स्तस्मिन्नेवतदाहनि ।
प्रतिपन्नं कलियुगं तस्यसंख्यानिबोधमे ॥

Kali Era is not a matter of guess work but is based on the solid foundations of Astronomical Science.

According to our Astronomical science, the seven planets 1. Saturn, 2. Jupitar, 3. Mars, 4. Sun, 5. Venus, 6. Mercury and 7. Moon should in conjunction (together) in the Mesha at the commencement of the Kali Era i. e., 5060 years back such a phenomenon occurred in 3102 B. C., at 2 hours 27 minutes and 30 seconds on 20 th February. The Kali Era reckoned from that moment. (This type of conjuction of the planets will recur again at the next such moment in the next Mahayuga in after 43, 20, 000 years).

The well known French Astronomer "Bailly" and others admitted that the conjunction of the planets described by our Hindu Astronomers occurred exactly correct to the minute and second at the time noted by them.

Prof. Count Bjornstjerna says :-

"According to the Astronomical calculations of the Hindus, the present period of the world, Kaliyuga commenced 3102 years before the birth of Christ, on the 20th February, at 2 hours 27 minutes and 30 seconds, the time being thus calculated to minutes and seconds. They say that a conjunction of the planets then took place, and their tables show this conjunction. Bailly states that Jupiter and Mercury were there in the same degree of the ecliptic, Mars at a distance of only eight, and saturn of seven degrees; whence it follows, that at the point of time given by the Brahmins as the commencement of Kaliyuga, the four planets above mentioned must have been successively concealed by the rays of the sun (First Saturn, then Mars, afterwards Jupiter and lastly Mercury). They thus showed themselves in conjunction; and although Venus, could not then be seen, it was natural to say that a conjunction of the planets then took place. The calculations of the Brahmins is so exactly confirmed by our own astronomical tables, that nothing but an actual observation could have given so correspondent a result. (Vide Hindu Superiority P. P. 283-284 by Har Bilas Sarada, third edition 1922.)

## PANCHANGAS (ANNUAL CALENDARS)

All the Panchangas (Native Annual Calendars) in vogue in the different parts of Bharat in which the positions and movements of the different planets and stars on the Zodiac during the year are recorded and their influence on the lives of human beings are predicted, have all been prepared year after year from times immemorial, and from the entrance of Kali reckoning the time on the Kali Era and adding up year after year. The Kali Era is the basis of all reckoning of time in these calendars.

In the calendars for the current year "VIKARI" of A. D. 1959 it will be found stated that 5060 years have gone by since the Kaliyuga commenced. The Mahabharata War is to be dated 36 years previous, to the advent of Kali ie., 5060 years back ie., 5060 - 1958 A. D. = 3138 B. C. This is the direct determination of the date of the Mahabharata War on the basis of our Native Annual Calendars, which form a National Institution in our country.

* * * *

# AGE OF THE MAHABHARATA WAR

## TOPIC - V.

### THE SAPTARSHI ERA

In a native historical treatise, the 'Kali Yuga Raja Vrittanta' (history of the kings of the Kali Yuga) it is stated :

श्लो ॥ यदायुधिष्टिरोराजा शक्रप्रस्थे प्रतिष्ठितः ।
तदासप्तर्षयः प्रापुर्मघाः पितृहितेरताः ॥

" पंचसप्ततिवर्षाणि प्राक्कलेः सप्ततेद्विजाः ।
मघास्वसन् महाराजे शासत्युर्वीं युधिष्टिरे ॥

"When Yudhishtira was crowned King at Indraprastha, over his half of Kaurava kingdom carved out for the Pandavas, the Constellation of the Great Bear or the Saptarshi Mandala entered the region of the star Magha, in the Zodiac." and again;

"Seventy five years before the commencement of the Kali Yuga, the Great Bear crossed over into Magha i. e., in B. C. (3102 + 75 =) 3177. Yudhishtira's reign at Indraprastha therefore commenced in B. C, 3177. The 75 years of his reign before Kali include 25 years of Suzerainty (Emperorship) over the whole of Bharat, which he enjoyed after the performance of the Rajasuya, the 13 years of exile as a consequence of his defeat in the game of Dice, 38 years on the whole, and the demand for the restoration of his kingdom as per the terms of the game at the end of the 13 years of exile, the refusal of Duryodhana to comply with the demand, and the War in 3138 B. C., the coronation of Yudhishtira again after the War as the undisputed Emperor of Bharat and the establishment of the Yudhishtira Era, 35 years of his rule after the War and the demise of Sri Krishna, the advent of Kali, his renunciation of the kingdom, entrusting it to Parikshit and starting on the Great Journey. in 3101 B. C., and there after it is stated :

श्लो ॥ पंचविंशतिवर्षेंषु गतेष्वथ कलौयुगे ।
समाश्रयिष्यं त्याश्लेषां, मुनयस्तेशतंसमाः ॥

"After the passage of 25 years in the Kali Yuga i. e., in B. C., (3102 - 25) 3077, the Great Bear in its retrograde motion, passes on from Magha to Aslesha and remain in it for a hundred years."

and :

श्लो ॥ तदैवधर्मपुत्रोऽपि महाप्रस्थान मास्थितः ।
भुवंपरिभ्रमन्नंते स्वर्गमारोक्ष्यतिधृवम् ॥

"Then i. e., in B. C. 3077, Yudhishtira, after completing the Great Journey or Pilgrimage round the world, ascends to heaven.

and :

श्लो ॥ तदैवलौकिकाब्दोऽपि सप्तविंश शतात्मकः ।
धर्मपुत्रज्ञापकार्थं लोकेतावत्प्रवर्तितः ॥

"Even then, i. e, in B. C. 3077 - 76 was inaugurated in memory of Yudhishtira, the Secular Era variously called "Laukikabda," Saptarshimana, Yudhishtira Swargarohana Kala, the Kashmirabda, of a duration of 2700 years.

From the account thus available to us in the Kaliyuga - Raja - Vrittanta,' the dates of four well-known events are athoritatively fixed for as

1. The entry of the Great Bear into Magha .... .... 3177 B. C.
2. The time of the Mahabharata War or Yudhishtira Era. .... 3138 B. C.
3. The commencement of the Kali Yuga .... .... .... 3102 B. C.
4. The inaguration of the Saptarashi Era, or Yudhshtira Swargarohana Kala, or Laukikabda or Kashmirabda .... .... .... .... .... .... 3076 B. C.

The fourth of these, called 'Laukikabda' because it was established by the people, Yudhishtira Kala, as it was established in memory of Yudhishtira's Swargarohana Kala, and Kashmirabda as it has been in vogue in Kashmir all along and used by the almanac makers as the basis of their calculations from year to year.

Kalhana, the author of the history of Kashmir, known as Raja Tarangini, has used this Laukikabda as the basis of his chronology.

Dr. Buhler the well-known European Historian himself has admitted the antiquity of this Laukikabda and the validity of the recognition of its starting point Kali 1 as equivalent to B. C. 3101.

"I do not doubt for a moment, that the calculation which throws the beginning of the Saptarshi Era back to 3076 B. C., is worth no more than that which fixes the beginning of the Kali Yuga in 3101 B. C. But it seems to me certain that it is much older than Kalhana's time, because his equation 24 = 1070 agrees with it. It may therefore be safely used for reducing with exactness the Saptarshi years, months and days mentioned in his work to years of the Christian Era. The results which will be thus obtained will always closely agree with those gained by Gen. Cunningham, who, did use the right key". (Vide pp 264-268 Indian Antiquary Vol VI of 1877 and p. 27 ff of Vol V of the Edn. — 1876.) Besides Dr. Buhler himself quotes the following verse in evidence of the currency of the Saptarshi Era in Kashmir.

श्लो ॥ कलेर्गतैः सायक नेत्रवर्षैः युधिष्ठिराद्याः त्रिदिवंप्रयाताः ।
लोकेहि संवत्सरपत्रिकायां सप्तर्षिमानं प्रवदंति संतः ॥

"After 25 years passed away in Kali, Yudhishtira and his brothers ascended to heaven." Dr. Buhler has interpolated in the above verse "सप्तर्षिवर्याः" "Saptarshivaryah" in the place of "युधिष्ठिराद्याः" "Yudhishtiradyah". But the emendation leads to no sensible meaning for the verse. For, the Saptarshis are always in heaven. There is no sense in stating that they will be in heaven in Kali 25. It is certainly sensible and meaningful to say, according to the other reading, that Yudhishtira and his brothers who had been on the earth since 75 years before Kali ascended to heaven, or passed away from the earth, in Kali 25. This is the version in the Puranas too. Dr. Buhler has effected the emendation on his own authority, deliberately render the verse consistent with the verse similarly interpolated by him (1-51) in Kalhana's Rajatarangini, stating that the Kurus and the Pandavas were all in existence in Kali 653. If it is established that Yudhishtira and his brothers passed away in 25 Kali, the statement in the verse interpolated by the 1-51. of the Rajatarangini stands directly contradicted by it. So, it is clear the emendation of "युधिष्ठराद्याः" "Yudhishtiradhyah" into "सप्तर्षिवर्याः" "Saptarshivaryah" was necessary for him to justify the other interpolation in the Rajatarangini (1-51). The Saptarshis of the constellation were never on the earth. They were manifested on the heavens at the beginning of the creation of the Universe or Srishti along with the other stars and planets and they will disappear from the heavens only at the time of 'Laya' or total destruction of the Universe. The planets of the existing universe are in their mid-career. They will endure for another 220 crores of years according to our Astronomical Science. To say that the Saptarishis reached heaven or passed away from the earth in Kali 25 is manifestly absurd. Hence the correct reading of the verse is with "युधिष्ठिराद्याः" "Yudhishtiradyah" and not "सप्तर्षिवर्याः" "Saptarshivaryah."

In the almanacs in vogus in Kashmir of the successive years, it is the "सप्तर्षिमान" "Saptarshi-mana" that is used for all determinations of time.

From the above statements of Dr. Buhler himself it is clear he has admitted Kali 1 = B. C. 3101, Saptarshi = Kali 26 = B. C. 3076. His admissions that the Great Bear, the Saptarshi Mandala which enterd Magha in 3177 - 76 B. C, and that the Era established after their entry into the next star 'Aslesha' begins in B. C. 3076, reveal clearly that he was aware of the stay of the saptarshi in Magha for the hundred years from B. C. 3177 - 76 to B. C. 3077 - 76, the statements in the Puranas which describe the reign of Yudhishtira as extending over the century, and the verses 13-3, of the 'Brihatsamhita' and 1-56 in Kalhana's Rajatarangini. So he knew that the time of the Mahabharata War is 3138 B. C. But knowingly the Western Orientalists kept back the truth.

* * * *

# AGE OF THE MAHABHARATA WAR

## TOPIC - VI.

### ASTRONOMICAL EVIDENCE

#### Brihatsamhita of Varahamihira

The Astronomer Varahamihiracharya refers in verse 3 of chapter XIII of his 'Brihatsamhita' to the reign of Yudhishtira, his ascent to the heavens, and the Saka Era in vogue in his time. The same verse was reproduced by Kalhana as the 56th verse in the 1st chapter of his 'Rajatarangini' and used by him to bring into mutual relation the time of the ascent to heaven of Emperor Yudhishtira, which was the basis of the chronological reckonings in his history, the Saka Era in vogue in the time of Varahamihira, the period of Yudhishtira's reign, and the movement of the constellation of the Great Bear.

The same Era based on the ascent to heaven of Emperor Yudhishtira is other wise variously referred to as Laukikabda, Yudhistirakala, Saptarshimana and Kashmirabda.

Brihatsamhita XIII-3 or Rajatarangini I-56 reads :

श्लों ।। आसन् मघासु मुनयः शासति पृथ्वीं युधिष्ठिरे नृपतौ ।
षड्द्विकपंचद्वियुत श्शककालः तस्यराज्ञश्च ।।

Which means :

The Saptarshis were in Magha during the reign of Yudhishtira. The (Swargarohana's) time of

Yudhishtira coupled with 2526 (years) becomes Saka-Kala. In the above verse the first line is plain. The ellipsis in the second line has to be filled up thus:

श्लो ॥ "तस्यत्र (युधिष्ठिरस्यच) राज्ञः (कालः=स्वर्गारोहण कालः)
षड्द्विक पंचद्वियुत (स्सन्), शककालः (भवति)"

"The Swargarohana time of Yudhishtira coupled with 2526 becomes Sakakalah." The Saptarshi Mandala, or the constellation of the Great Bear passed over from the region of the star Magha into that of the next, in Kali 26. That was the beginning of the Era variously known as Saptarshimana, or Yudhishtira Kala, or Laukikabda, or Kashmirabda. The Era known as Saka Era, in vogue in Varahamihira's time began in Kali 26 plus 2526 or Kali 2552 or B. C. (3102-2552) 550. Varaha, in his endeavour to fix unambiguously the starting point of the Saka Era in vogue in his time, first laid down the contemporaneity of the Saptarshimandala in Magha (an astronomical event) and the period of Yudhishtira's reign on the earth. Then he stated that the Saka Era began 2526 years after the commencement of the 'Yudhishtirakala' i. e., the years of Yudhishtira's ascent to heaven (Kali 26).

But there is no reference whatever in his verse to the Salivahana Saka and no evidence of any kind to indicate, as the modern Orientalists of the European School choose to take for granted, that by "Sakakala" he meant the Salivahana Saka.

If we suppose that Varaha referred to the Salivahana Saka in his verse, since the Salivahana Saka is agreed on all hands to begin in Kali 3179, he would have given 3153 years from the Swargarohana Kala of Yudhishtira (i. e., Kali 26). But he gave only 2526 years as the distance from Yudhishtira Kala (Kali 26) to his Sakakaala, i. e., Kali 26 + 2526 = 2552 of Kalisaka. Therefore, there must be another Saka Kala which was in existence in his time. So, we have to take into consideration only that particular 'Saka Kala of 2552 Kali but not the Salivahana Saka of 3179 Kali.

Varaha has fixed the time of Yudhishtira's reign in the first line of the verse as the time when the Saptarshis were in Magha. As regards the time when the Saptarshi Mandala was in Magha, Bhattotpala, in his commentary on Varahamihira's Brihatsamhita XIII-3, quoted the statement of Vriddhagarga "कलिद्वापरसंधौतु स्थितास्ते पितृदैवतम्" "Kali Dwapara Samdhautu Sthitasthe Pitrudaivatam" as the authority. "Kalidwapara sandhi" means the turning point when the Dwapara-Yuga came to a close and the Kali-Yuga began. It happened 36 years after the Mahabharata War and at hrs 2-27"-30" on the 20th of February, in the year B. C. 3102, according to the unanimous opinion of Western as well as Eastern Scholars. This has never been disputed by any. That the Great Bear was then in Magha has been unanimously declared by the Astronomers and the authors of the Puranas of ancient Bharat.

The opinion of Dr. Buhler has been quoted. General Alexander Cunningham has, in his note under the caption "Saptarshi Saka" on page 17 in his publication "Indian Eras" given a table showing the star-region in which the Saptarshi Mandala is found in each century from B. C. 5877 to A. D. 2125, according to which it was in Magha from B. C. 3177 to B. C. 3077. The table is reproduced at the end of the discussion in this Topic VI-for reference. It should clear all the doubts and misconceptions of the modern historians. Dr. Cunningham's table agrees with the statements of Vriddha Garga, Varahamihira, Bhattotpala and other ancient Indian Scholars. It is thus proved 75 years previous to the advent of Kali in B. C. 3102 i. e., in B, C. 3177 the Saptarshi Mandala entered the region of Magha. The same year Yudhishtira was crowned King of the Pandava's share of the Kaurava Dominions, with his capital at Indraprastha, according to the Puranas the relevant statements from which have been reproduced in chapter V.

It is established indisputably that the Saptarshi Mandala was in Magha from B. C. 3177-76 to B. C. 3077-76. Yudhishtira also was crowned king at Indraprastha in B. C. 3177, gradually extended his Empire and performed the Rajasuya and established himself as the Emperor of Bharat and in B. C. 3151 he lost his Empire in the game of Dice with his cousin and remained in exile for 13 years thereafter, that is till B. C. 3138, and in B. C. 3138 waged the Great War known as the Mahabharata War, in which he emerged victorious and once again established himself as the

Emperor of Bharat; and in B. C. 3102 Mahabharata War i.e. 3102, having learnt of the Niryana of Sri Krishna and the advent of Kali, renounced his Empire and started on a tour to all the holy places of pilgrimage and finally in B.C. 3077, ascended to haven. From the first line in the verse of Varahamihira (XIII-3 of his Brihat Samhita), it is stated that the period of Yudhishtira's rule extended from B. C. 3177-76 to B. C. 3077-76 and the Saptarshi's were then in Magha. In the second line of the same verse it is stated that by the addition of 2526 to the Swargarohana Kala i. e. B. C. 3076 of Yudhishtira we get the Saka-Kala in vogue in his time. That is Kali 26 + 2526 = Kali 2552 or B. C. 3076-2526 = B. C. 550 is the beginning of the Saka Era in vogue in Varaha's time. There is no conjecture or interpretation of our own in this calculation. It is based on the statements of Varahamihira himself. We have thus been able to establish the Magha century of the Saptarshi's from B. C. 3177-76 to 3077-76 B. C. and the starting point of the Yudhishtira Kala B. C. 3076 as well as the Saka Era of Varaha is B. C. 550. To conjecture that the Saka Era mentioned by Varaha is the Salivahana Saka and to twist the meaning of the verse to suit the conjecture is absolutely unwarranted.

Varahamihira indicates his own time in his Pancha Siddhantika in the line "सप्ताश्वि वेदसंख्यं शककालमपास्य" "Saptasvi Veda Samkhym Saka Kala mapasya" which means that he was writing in the year 427 of the Saka Era i. e., in Kali 2552 plus 427 = 2979 Kali. So Varaha belongs to 2979 Kali or B. C. 3102-2979 = B. C. 123. To fix his time as 427 on the Salivahana Saka or (78+427) A. D. 505 is obviously wrong. The year B. C. 123 as Varahas's time agrees with the tradition that he adorned the court of Vikramaditya who ruled as the Emperor of Bharat from Kali 3020 or B. C. 82 to Kali 3120 or A. D. 19 and established a new Era of his own, the Vikrama Era, in Kali 3044 or B. C. 57.

Rao Bahadur P. V. Kane, High Court Vakil Bombay and President of the Indian History congress in 1953 interprets the verse in yet another original manner. He holds that the two lines of the verse XIII-3 of the Brihatsamhita give us two independent sentences; that in the first Varahamihira reproduces in his own words the statement of Vriddhagarga that while Yudhishtira was reigning (from B. C. 3177 to 3077) the Saptarshi Mandala was in the star Magha; and in the second line Varaha gives us his own rule (principle) that by the addition of 2526 to the year on the Salivahana Era (which began in 78 A. D.) we get the year (time of Yudhishtira). We reproduce his interpretation in his own words below.

"The verse (Br.S. 13.3) contains two independent clauses in the two halves of it, viz. namely 1. The constellation of the seven sages was in the Maghas when Yudhishtira ruled over the earth as king and secondly the Saka Kala increased by 2526 years represents the time of that king." In the first half of XIII-3 and in several other verses of the same chapter (viz. verses 7 to 11) Varaha states in Arya verses Vriddhagarga's views (which were in the Anustuph metre, as the quotations given by Utpala from Vriddhagarga will show) in his own words and in the second half he states his own view about the Yudhishtira Era.

The particle 'ca' is added because the two halves are two independent sentences and the second half comes to this 'Shad dwika panca dwi yutah saka kalah thasya rajnah (kalah, understood from the preceding word Saka-Kalah). (vide journal of the Andhra Historical Reasearch Society, Rajahmundry, Vol. XX Narayanarao Memorial Volume 1954' and p 75 of Ancient Hindu History pt. II by this author.)

Let us agreo for a moment to this curious interpretation of the learned Sri Kane. Then it means Varaha quoted Vriddagarga's opinion only to reject it and to offer his own. There is no warrant for such an assumption anywhere in the verse or in the whole treatise, or anywhere else in the tradition of Indian Scholarship. It is entirely due to the distorted vision of the learned Sri Kane himself due to his anxiety to justify the statement that the Kauravas and Pandavas were alive in Kali 653 or B. C. 2448 in the I-51 verse of Kalhana's Rajatarangini. (which was itself an interpolation by Dr. Buhler.)

But there is no reason arose of any kind to take the two lines of the verse of Varaha as independent statements, or that the Saka-Kala referred to by him is the Salivahana Saka-Kala. On the other hand "तस्यराज्ञश्च" "Thasya Rajnascha" in the second clause is manifestly based on the first. Varaha starts with fixing the time of Yudhishtira's reign in the century from B. C. 3177 to B. C. 3077, and proceeds to fix the beginning of the Saka Era in vogue in his time at 2526 years after the year of the ascent of Yudhishtira to heaven towards the end of the century of his reign (in B. C 3077-76 or Kali 26) i. e., B. C. 3076-2526 = B. C. 550. This determination is accepted as such by Kalhana in I-55 of his Rajatarangini as the determination of the Samhitakaras based on the movement of the constellation of the seven sages (तच्चारे संहिता कारैः एवं दत्तोऽत्र निर्णयः") and as the authoritative basis for the chronology of his history and then in his I-56 reproduces verbatim XIII-3 of the Brihatsamhita of Varaha-mihira. There is no indication in Kalhana's writings that there was any difference of opinion among the ancient samhitakaras 'Vriddha-garga' and 'Varahamihira'.

In the commentary on Varahamihira's Brihatsamhita written by Bhattotpala, he did not give any indication that there was difference of opinion between 'Varaha' and 'Vriddha-Garga'. In addition, he quoted the view-point of Vriddha-Garga to strengthen the opinion of Varaha. Therefore the imaginary views of the learned Sri Kane are contrary to the view-points of Kalhana, Vriddha-Garga, Varaha and Bhattotpala. They are also contrary to the views expressed by Alexander cunningham and Dr. Buhler and what has been stated in Puranas and Mahabharata.

Let us follow Bhattotpala's commentary on XIII-3 of Brihat samhita :—

"मुनयो मरीच्यादय: सप्तर्षयो, युधिष्ठिरे पांडुतनये, नृपतौ राजानि, पृथ्वीं महीं, शासयति परिपालयति, मघासु मघानक्षत्रेषु आसन् अध्यस्थिष्ठन्"

"Munayo Marichyaadayah Saptarshayo, Yudhistire Pandutanayo, Nrupathau Raajani, Pridhviim Mahiim, Saasati paripalayati, Maghaasu Magha-Nakshathreshu, Aasan adhyathishtan". "When Yudhishtira was the ruling monarch on the earth the sages were in Magha." "तथाहि वृद्धगर्ग:" "Thadhahi Vriddha Gargah"-means 'Vruddha Garga also says in the same way'; and and he quotes the same words of 'Vruddha Garga' "कलिद्वापर संधौतु स्थितास्ते पितृदैवतम्" "Kali Dwaapara sandhautu sthitaaste pithru daivatam" means "at the transition age of Dwapara into Kali, the seven sages were in the Magha star." Then Bhattotpala proceeds with his commentary thus :- "तस्यच युधिष्ठिरस्यच राज्ञ: षड्द्विक पंचद्वियुत: शककालोगत:" "Tasyacha Yudhishtirasya Raajnah shadwika pancha dviyutah (2526) sakakaalo (427) gatah", which means in the (Swargarohana) kala of Ydhistira elapsed 2526 coupled with Saka-nrupakaala (427), 'एवमृकृतेयद्भवति तावद्वर्षं वृन्दं वर्तमानकालं यावत् गतम्" "Evam Krute Yadbhavati taavadvarsha brundam varthamaana kaalam yaavat gatham" means :- when calculated in this manner the total amount of years (i. e., Kali 26 plus 2526 plus 427 = 2979 (years) will be the period that elapsed from the commencement of Kali 1 to the time of the writing of Brihatsamhita by Varahamihira. (i.e., 3102 B. C. minus 2979 Kali =). 123 B. C. Therefore, according to Bhattotpala, the Sakakala of Varaha in XIII-3, of his Brihatsamhita is 427 of Sakanrupakaala but not A. D. 78 plus 427 = 505 A. D. of Salivahana. According to the interpretation of the learned Kane, also "Sakakala increased by 2526 represents Yudhishtira Kalah", means Sakanrupakaalah 427 plus 2526 = 2953 of Yudhishtira Kaala. (Yudhishtira Kala's beginning B. C. 3076—2953 = B. C. 123 the time of Varaha).

N. B. Beginning of Sakanrupakaala is (B. C. 26+2526 = ) 2552 Kali and the beginning of Salivahana Saka-Kaala is 3179 Kali.

On the other hand he adopts their agreed opinion as his own. Thus it is clear from Kalhana's I-56 which is but a quotation of the same as well as XIII-3, of the Brihatsamhita of Varahamihira that the time of ascent of Yudhishtira to heaven or the beginning of the Laukikabda is in B. C. 3076, the beginning of the Saka Era in vogue in Varaha's time is in 2552 Kali, or B. C. 550 and that the period of Yudhishtira's reign lasted from B. C. 3177 to B. C. 3077 and in that Century the time of the Mahabharata War is 36 years before Kali or B. C. 3138.

* * * *

11)

Let us follow Bhattotpala's commentary on XIII-3 of Brihat samhita :–

"मुनयो मरीच्यादयः सप्तर्षयो, युधिष्ठिरे पांडुतनये, नृपतौ राजानि, पृथ्वीं महीं, शासयति परिपालयति, मघासु मघानक्षत्रेषु आसन् अध्यस्थिष्ठन्"

"Munayo Marichyaadayah Saptarshayo, Yudhistire Pandutanayo, Nrupathau Raajani, Pridhviim Mahiim, Saasati paripalayati, Maghaasu Magha-Nakshathreshu, Aasan adhyathishtan". "When Yudhishtira was the ruling monarch on the earth the sages were in Magha." "तथाहि वृद्धगर्गः" "Thadhahi Vriddha Gargah"-means 'Vruddha Garga also says in the same way'; and and he quotes the same words of 'Vruddha Garga' "कलिद्वापर संधौतु स्थितास्ते पितृदैवतम्" "Kali Dwaapara sandhautu sthitaaste pithru daivatam" means "at the transition age of Dwapara into Kali, the seven sages were in the Magha star." Then Bhattotpala proceeds with his commentary thus :- "तस्यच युधिष्ठिरस्यच राज्ञः षड्द्विक पंचद्वियुतः शककालोगतः" "Tasyacha Yudhishtirasya Raajnah shadwika pancha dviyutah (2526) sakakaalo (427) gatah", which means in the (Swargarohana) kala of Ydhistira elapsed 2526 coupled with Saka-nrupakaala (427), 'एवम्कृतेयद्भवति तावद्वर्षं वृन्दं वर्तमानकालं यावत् गतम्" "Evam Krute Yadbhavati taavadvarsha brundam varthamaana kaalam yaavat gatham" means :- when calculated in this manner the total amount of years (i. e., Kali 26 plus 2526 plus 427 = 2979 (years) will be the period that elapsed from the

| | | | | | | | | | |
|---|---|---|---|---|---|---|---|---|---|
| 13. | Purva Bhadrapada | 1538 | 4677 | 1132 | 1977 | 3862 | 725 | Jyeshtha | 13. |
| 14. | Satabhisha | 1438 | 4577 | 1262 | 1877 | 3962 | 825 | Anuradha | 14. |
| 15. | Dhanishtha | 1338 | 4477 | 1362 | 1777 | 4062 | 925 | Visakha | 15. |
| 16 | Sravana | 1238 | 4377 | 1462 | 1677 | 4162 | 1025 | Svati | 16. |
| 17. | Uttara Ashadha | 1138 | 4277 | 1562 | 1577 | 4262 | 1125 | Chittra | 17. |
| 18. | Purva Ashadha | 1038 | 4177 | 1662 | 1477 | 4362 | 1225 | Hastha | 18. |
| 19. | Mula | 938 | 4077 | 1762 | 1377 | 4462 | 1325 | Uttara Phalguni | 19. |
| 20. | Jyeshta | 838 | 3977 | 1862 | 1277 | 4562 | 1425 | Purva Phalguni | 20. |
| 21. | Anuradha | 738 | 3877 | 1962 | 1177 | 4662 | 1525 | Magha | 21. |
| 22. | Visakah | 638 | 3777 | 2062 | 1077 | 4762 | 1625 | Aslesha | 22. |
| 23. | Svati | 538 | 3677 | 2162 | 977 | 4362 | 1725 | Pushya | 23. |
| 24. | Chittra | 438 | 3577 | 2262 | 877 | 4962 | 1825 | Punarvasu | 24. |
| 25. | Hasta | 338 | 3477 | 2362 | 777 | 5062 | 1925 | Ardra | 25. |
| 26 | Uttara Phalguni | 238 | 3377 | 2462 | 677 | 5162 | 2025 | Mrigasiras | 26. |
| 27. | Purva Phalguni | 138 | 3277 | 2562 | 577 | 5262 | 2125 | Rohini | 27. |

# AGE OF THE MAHABHARATA WAR

## TOPIC - VII.

### WRONG CONJECTURES

At the time of the Mahabharata War, correctly determined, the Pandavas, Draupadi, Sri Krishna, the Kauravas, Bhishma, Drona and other Bharata Warriors must be in existence. It should be the transition time from Dwapara to Kali. The Constellation of the seven sages be in the star region of Magha. It has been admitted on all hands by the Astronomical Scholars of ancient Bharat, and the European Orientalists like Dr. Buhler and General Alexander Cunningham that the Constellation of the seven sages was in the Magha region from B. C. 3177 to B. C. 3077. The Astronomers and the authors of the Puranas of ancient Bharat, all unanimously declare that Yudhishtira was reigning during that century. That the ascent of Yudhishtira to heaven occurred in B. C. 3076 or Kali 26 when the Constellation passed over from Magha to the next star, is conceded By Dr. Buhler, Dr. Wilson and General Alexander Cunningham. How could Sri Krishna who passed away in B. C. 3102 and the Pandavas who passed away in B. C. 3077-76 be alive in B. C. 2448 or 1931, 1886, 1500, 1400, 1100, or 900 if any of the conjectures be correct, of the modern historians of Ancient Bharat, the Euopean Orientalists or their Indian disciples? How could the Constellation of the seven sages which was in Magha in B. C. 3177 to B. C. 3077-76, be in any of the years noted above? Is there any inscriptional or historical authority for their determination? Such determinations and arguments deserve only the contempt of genuine historians and competent scholars. The final result of all the above discussion is the time of the Mahabharata War is indisputably B. C. 3138, when the Saptarshimandala was in Magha century.

* * * *

# AGE OF THE MAHABHARATA WAR

## TOPIC - VIII.

### INSCRIPTIONAL EVIDENCE

There are four inscriptions, extant and available to us (apart from several others that might have been lost or destroyed), which prove conclusively that the Mahabharata War occurred in B. C. 3138 or 36 years before Kali. Of these four, two have been published in the Indian Antiquary. The third does not seem to have attracted the attention of the Government Archaeological Department. It has been copied from the person in possession of it and published recently at Masulipatam in the Krishna District. The fourth is the copper plate inscription of Emperor Suddhanva. The contents of these four inscriptions bear out the deterimination, without scope for any doubt, that the Mahabharata War occurred in B. C. 3138. It is hoped that this evidence at least will be respected by the Modern Indian historians and they will be able to reconstruct tho correct history of ancient Bharat on the basis of it.

Sri Krishna passed away in B. C. 3102 tho Kali Yuga commenced simultaneously. In Kali 1 or B. C. 3101 Yudhishtira renounced his Empire, installed Parikshit on the imperial throne and started with his brothers on the Mahaprasthana or the Great Journey. Parikshit reigned for 60 years and died due to snake-bite in B. C. 3041. His son Janamejaya was crowned in B. C. 3041. In the 29th year of his reign i.e., in B.C. 3013-3012 or Kali 89, in the year Plavanga on Monday the new - moonday at the end of Chaitra, he donated two villages to two religious institutions and the two gift-deeds were inscribed. One of these is found published in the pages 333, 334 of the Indian Antiquary. It reads as follows:

The First Inscription :

JANAMEJAYA'S GIFT DEED

"श्रीकुरुवंशावतंस श्रीजनमेजयभूपालनां दानशासनपत्रं ।

श्लो ॥ पांतु वो जलदश्यामाः शार्ङ्गज्याघातकर्कशाः ।
त्रैलोक्यमंडपस्तम्भाश्चत्वारो हरिबाहवः ॥ १

"स्वस्तिश्री जयाभ्युदये युधिष्ठिरशके प्लवंगाख्ये (ख्य) एकोननवती (८९)वत्सरे सहस्यमासि अमावास्यायां सोमवासरे श्रीमन्महाराजाधिराज-परमेश्वरो वैयघ्रणी वैयाघ्र (?) पाद गोत्रजः श्रीजनमेजयभूपः किष्किंधा-नगर्यां सिंहासनस्थः सकलवर्णाश्रमधर्मप्रतिपालकः पश्चिमदेशस्थसीतापुर-वृकोदरक्षेत्रे तत्रत्य मुनिबृन्द मठस्य गरुडवाहनतीर्थश्रीमच्छिष्यकैकचार्यै-राधितसीतारामस्य पूजार्थं कृतभूदान शासन मस्मत्प्रपितामहयुधिष्ठिरा-धिष्ठितमुनिव्रृन्दक्षेत्रस्य चतुःसीमापरिमितिक्रमः :—

"पूर्वभागे ......... उत्तरवाहिन्यास्तुंगभद्रयाः पश्चिमे दक्षिणभागे अगस्त्याश्रमसंगमादुत्तरे । पश्चिमे पाषाणनद्याः पूर्वे । उत्तरभागे च्छिन्न-नद्या दक्षिणे । ये (ए) तन्मध्यस्थितमुनिबृन्दक्षेत्रं भवच्छिष्यपारंपरा-चंद्रार्कपर्यंतं निधिनिक्षेपजल पाषाणाक्षिण्या (?) गामिसिद्धसाध्यतेजः स्वाम्यसहितं स्वबुध्याऽनुकूल्येनाऽस्मता पित्रूणां विष्णुलोकप्राप्त्यर्थं हरिहर-सन्निधावुपरागसमये सहिरण्येन तुङ्गभद्राजलाधारापूर्वकं क्षेत्रं यतिहस्ते दत्तो (त्तवान्, अ) (?) स्म्यहं । एतद्धर्मसाधनस्य साक्षिणः ॥

श्लो ॥ आदित्यचंद्रावनिलोऽनलश्च द्यौर्भूमिरापोहृदयं यमश्च ।
अहश्च रात्रिश्च उभे च संध्ये धर्मश्च जानाति नरस्य वृत्तं ॥ (२)

" दानपालनयोर्मध्ये दानाच्छ्रेयोऽनुपालनं ।
दानात्स्वर्गमवाप्नोति पालनादत्युत्तमं पदं ॥ (३)

" स्वदत्ताद्द्विगुणं पुण्यं परदत्तानुपालने ।
परदत्तापहारेण स्वदत्तं निष्फलं भवेत् ॥ (४)

" मद्दत्ता पुत्रिका ज्ञेया पितृदत्ता सहोदरी ।
अन्यदत्ता तु जननी दत्तभूमिं परित्यजेत ॥ (५)

" अन्यैस्तु छर्दितं छद्दे श्वभिश्च छर्दितं न तु ।
ततः कष्टो ततो नीचः स्वयं दत्तापहारकः ॥ (६)

" स्वदत्तां परदत्तां वा ब्रह्मवृत्ति हरेतयः ।
षष्ठिर्वर्षसहस्राणि विष्ठायां जायते कृमिः ॥ (७)

It is clearly stated in this inscription that the gift of land for the worship of Sitarama mentioned there in was made by Emperor Janamejaya in the year 89 of the Jayabhyudaya Yudhishtira Era. Jayabhyudaya Yudhishtira Saka is named after 'Jaya' "तथो जय मुदीरयेत्" "tatho 'Jaya' mudeerayet". The name by which Bhagavan Vyasa called his great epic as "Jaya" now known as "Mahabharata" which he began to compose in Kali 1, and completed in 3 years. Jayabhyudaya Yudhishtira Era 1 means therefore only Kali 1. Jayabhyudaya Yudhishtira Saka 89 means Kali 89 or B. .C (3101-89) = 3012. It was the 29th year of the reign of Emperor Janamejaya. He came to the throne on the death of his father Emperor Parikshit in Kali 60.

The Second Inscription :

A similar gift of land was made on the same day by the same Emperor Janamejaya for the worship of Kedaranathaswamy at the Kedara Kshetra, in the Himalayas to the head of the 'Usha-Matt', Sri Goswamy Ananda Linga Jangama Swamy through his disciple Sri Jnana Linga Jangama. The copper-Plate on which the gift deed is inscribed is preserved to this day in the same Matt. It does not seem to have reached the notice of the Government Archaeological Department. So it is not reported in the Indian Antiquari. A copy of it has been taken by some Andhra Pilgrims of the Saiva religious sect to the Saiva Shrine, and it has been published on their return home, at Masulipatam. The text of the inscription as published by them is given in his "Ancient Hindu History Part-I, by this Author. The same text is also given below :—

"स्वस्तिश्री जयाभ्युदययुधिष्ठिरशके प्लवंगाख्ये एकोननवतितम (८९) वत्सरे सहसिमासि अमावास्यायां सोमवासरे श्रीमन्महाराजाधिराजपरमेश्वर वैयाघ्रपदगोत्रज श्रीजनमेजयभूपो इंद्रप्रस्थनगरीसिंहासनस्थः सकलवर्णाश्रमधर्मंप्रतिपालको उत्तरहिमालये श्रीकेदारक्षेत्रं तत्रत्यमुनयः उषामठस्य श्रीगोस्वामिआनंदलिंगजंगमाय श्रीमच्छिष्यज्ञानलिङ्गजङ्गमद्वाराराधित-श्रीकेदारनाथस्य पूजार्थं दत्तवंतः चतुस्सीमा परिमितिक्रमः ॥ पूर्वंभागे दक्षिणवाहिनी मंदाकिनी। पश्चिमदक्षिणभागे क्षीरगंगा उत्तरपश्चिमे

13)

मधुगंगा, पूर्वोत्तरभागे स्वर्गद्वारनदी, दक्षिणे सरस्वती, मंदाकिन्योः संगमः, एतन्मध्ये श्रीकेदारक्षेत्रं भवच्छिष्यपरंपरया चंद्रार्कपर्यंतं निधिनिक्षेप जलपाषाणागामि सिद्धसाध्यतेजःस्वाम्यसहित मनुभोक्तुं स्वबुध्यानुकूल्ये नास्मन्मातृपितॄणां शिवलोकप्राप्त्यर्थं श्रीकेदारेश्वरसन्निध उपरागसमये सहिरण्यमंदाकिनी जलधारापूर्वकं क्षेत्रमिदं हस्ते दत्तवानस्मि । एतद्धर्मसाधनस्य साक्षिणः ।

श्लो ॥ आदित्यचंद्रावनिलोऽनलश्च । द्यौर्भूमिरापो हृदयं यमश्च ।
अहश्च रात्रिश्च उभे च संध्ये धर्मश्च जानाति नरस्य वृत्तं ॥(२)

" दानपालनयोर्मध्ये दानाच्छ्रेयोऽनुपालनं ।
दानात्स्वर्गमवाप्नोति पालनाद्द्विगुणं फलं ॥ (३)

" स्वदत्ता पुत्रिका ज्ञेया पितृदत्ता सहोदरी ।
अन्यदत्तातु जननी दत्तभूमिं परित्यजेत् ॥ (४)

" स्वदत्तां परदत्तांवा ब्रह्मवृत्ति हरेतयः ।
षष्ठिवर्षसहस्राणि विष्ठायां जायते कृमिः ॥ (५)

The above two inscriptions record two gifts of land by the Emperor Janamejaya at the time of the Solar eclipse on the same day. In the first the Donar is described as seated on the imperial throne at the city of Kishkindha and in the second as seated on the imperial throne at the city of Indra-prastha. The discrepancy may give rise to some doubts. Janamejaya was crowned Emperor of Bharat at Indra-prastha, the imperial capital. But it was the custom in ancient as in modern times, to celebrate the coronation of the Emperor simultaneously in all the chief cities, of the Empire. So it was the tradition to describe him in a gift-deed as the Emperor seated on the throne at the chief city of that province in which the land gifted away was situated. Kishkindha was the capital of the South Western province of the Empire. So he was described as "किष्किंध नगर्याम् सिम्हासनस्थः" "Kishkindha Nagaryam simhasanasthah" in the gift-deed relating to the land in that province and as "इंद्रप्रस्थ नगरे सिम्हसनस्थः" "Indraprastha Nagare simhasanasthah" in the gift-deed relating to the land in the Himalayan region.

Janamejaya was crowned at Indraprastha only. The two gifts were made at Indraprastha only. But the narration in the gift-deed was appropriately worded in view of the location of the land gifted. The apparant discrepancy need not give rise to any doubts of the authenticity of the gifts or the deeds or the inscriptions.

The Third Inscription :

## THE AIHOLE INSCRIPTION

There is an inscription on the walls of a temple of Siva in the village 'Iballi' in the Dharwar district. The date of the inscription is stated in the same. It states further that by the year 556 on the Saka Era, (or 634 of the Christian Era) the time that elapsed in Kali, after the Mahabharata War is 37 + 3735. The inscription was carved by the direction of king

Pulakesin II in A.D. 634. It was this Pulakesin who defeated and checked the Southward progress of the conquering armies of Sri Harsha Siladitya on the banks of the Krishna. His heroic, exploits, his victory in the battle with Sri Harsha, the other princes defeated by him are all described in the inscription. The inscription in its entirety has been published on pages 67-71 of the volume V of the Indian Antiquary. Modern historians have been attaching very great importance te this inscription as it gives a detailed account of Pulakesin II to whom there is no reference at all in the Puranas.

The same inscription has been also published as the 16th document in Vol. No. 34 of the Kaavya-mala series, under the caption 'Silalekha' or 'Stone inscription' of Pulakesin II of the Chalukya dynasty. (Vide pages 68-72 of Pt. I of Prachina Lekha Mala).

This inscription is all in Sanskrit. The author of this volume. who has already published another volume entitled "Ancient Hindu History part II, (Archaeological evidence misused"), who was known, before he took Holy orders, by the name of Sri Kota Venkatachelam, Gandhinagaram, Vijayawada and is known now, after assuming the ochre vobes as "Advayanamda Sankara Bharati Jagadguru Swami, (Srimadabhinava Virupaksha Peetadhipati)" had occassion to study the facsimile text of the inscription published in the Indian Antiquary and also learnt the process of deciphering the letters of the inscription, with the help of Sri Rallabhandi Subbarao Pantulu, M. A., B. Ed., retired Professor of History in the Government Arts College at Rajahmundry and Honourary Secretary of the Andhra Historical Research Society, Rajahmundry. Thus he could acquire first hand-knowledge of the text of the inscription. Here is the portion of the text giving the date of the inscription.

श्लो ॥ त्रिंशत्सु त्रिसहस्रेषु भारतादाहवादितः ।
सप्ताब्दशतयुक्तेषु (ग) शतेष्वब्देषु पंचसु ।

पंचाशत्सु कलौकाले षट्सु पंचशतासुच ।
समासु समतीतासु शकानामपि भूभुजाम् ॥

which means: From the Mahabharata War, and after 30 + 3000 + 700 + 500 years passed by, in Kali and 50 + 6 + 500 years after the destruction of the Saka kings, on the advise of the scholar Ravikirthi, this temple of Jinendra has been constructed (by Pulakesin II). Dr. Fleet, conceding that three Eras are referred to in the inscription, interprets it thus:- First he translates the text of the inscription as follows: Vide P 73, of Vol V of the Indian Antiquary, "Three thousand seven hundred and thirty years having elapsed since the War of the Bharatas and (three thousand) five hundred and fifty years having elapsed in the Kali Age, and five hundred and six years of the Saka kings having elapsed, this stone temple of Jinendra the abode of glory, was constructed by the order of the learned Ravikirthi etc., etc.,

14)

According to his interpretation

(1) The time of the Mahabharata War works out to 3730 – (506 on the Saka Era or) 584 of the Christian era = 3146 B.C. only approximately to the correct figure 3138 B. C.

(2) The time of the beginning of Kali works out to 3550 – (506 on the Saka Era or) 584 of the Christian era = B.C. 2966. This is in utter contradiction to the determination of B.C. 3102 unanimously accepted by the Artsonomers and Historical Scholars of the East as well as the West.

(3) Dr. Fleet equates the Saka year 506 with 584 A. D., as the time of the inscription. But Pulakesin II belongs to Saka 556 or A. D. 634 and not A. D. 584. So his interpretation cannot be accepted as it leads to wrong results to the three Eras.

The interpretation attempted in the Kavyamala series is even more outrageous. There it is conjectured that there are mistakes in the inscription and two corrections are suggested in line 2 of the portion of the inscription given above. They suggest the correction of

(1) "सप्ताब्द शत" "Saptabda Sata" into "सहाब्दशत" "Sahabdasata" and

(2) "शतेष्वब्देषु" "Sateshwabdeshu" into "गतेष्वब्देषु" "Gateshwabdeshu". According to these corrections and the interpretations based on them:—

By Salivahana 556 or A. D. 634, 30 + 3000 + 100 + 5 = 3135 years have passed since the Mahabharata War and the advent of Kali. The Mahabharata War and the advent of Kali are dated B. C. 2501. This is not acceptable as the date of the Mahabharata War or of the advent of Kali to any school of Historians or Astronomers. So it is clear the correction does not mend wrong.

The author's interpretation is as follows :—The text reads – "From the Mahabharata War (37 years upto the advent of Kali, and the period 30 + 3000 + 700 + 500 = 4230 years after the advent of Kali and 50 + 6 + 500 or 556 years of the Saka Era. (or Salivahana Saka Era).

Salivahana Era 556 = A. D. 634 time of Mahabharata War works out to 4230 – 634 = B. C. 3596, which is unacceptable. So there must be some mistake somewhere. But the two corrections suggested by the Kaavya Maala Publisheres are not necessary. One slight correction will do to yield a plausible interpretation for the whole inscription. That is to correct "शतेष्वब्देषु पंचसु" "Sateshwadeshu Panchasu" into "गतेष्वब्देषु पंचसु" Gateshwabdeshu Panchasu". (In the script of the inscription the letter "ग" "Ga" is similar to the letter "स" "Sa"). Then the inscription reads :- "From the Mahabhrata War to the advent of Kali elapsed 37 years + (30 + 3000 + 700 + 5) or 3735 hsve passed by 556 of the Saka Era or 634 of the Christian Era.

(1) So the time of the Mahabharata War then works out to 37 + 3735 = 3772 – before Saka 556 or A. D. 634 = B. C. 3138.

(2) Time of advent of Kali = 3735 years before 634 A. D. = 3101 B. C

(3) Saka 556 = A. D. 634 the time of Pulakesin II.

It is possible the "ग" "Ga" was corrected into "श" "Sa" by some interested party at the time of the discovery of the inscription before its publication. This has to be carefully investigated, for the rest the inscription is clear.

The Fourth Inscription :

### THE COPPER PLATE INSCRIPTION OF EMPEROR "SUDHANVA."

This inscription was inscribed by Sudhanva, who ruled over Guzarat. He was an Emperor with some tributary rulers under him. He reigned in the 5th Century before Christ. While Sri Adi Sankara was touring in the Western regions of Bharat, carrying on his glorious campaign against the heterodox religious school of thought like the Buddha, the Jaina and the Kapalika, a historic assembly of religious leaders (of all denominations of religion) was held under the auspices of this Emperor Sudhanva. All the religious leaders unanimously elected the Emperor to preside over the discussions and to decide the victor in the controversies. There Sri Sankara was able to refute the arguments and defeat the exponents of all the heterodox religions one after another. Thus more than a thousand religions including

Bauddha and Jaina were disproved and condemned by Sri Adi Sankara with irrefutable arguments. The Sanatana dharma, based on the authority of the Vedas was declared the victor and the only true religion by the president Sudhanva who was also the Judge. He had been an adherent of the Jaina religion. But now, that all his doubts had been cleared, he renounced his adherence to the Jaina religion, and overwhelmed with wonder at the vast erudection and profound philosophical wisdom of Sri Sankara, he sought refuge with the great religious truth from him. A memorandom presented by that Emperor Sndhanva to Sri Sankara was inscribed on copper-plate and this inscription was first published by Sri Kanuparti Markandeya Sarma in his Biography (published in 1928). It has copied from that publication by Sri Mudigonda Venkata Rama Sastry and obtained by the author from the latter and now republished below. It is not known whether it has found place in the pages of the Indian Antiquary.

Text of Inscription :-

"श्री महाकालनाथाय नमः – श्री महाकाल्यै नमः"

"श्रीमत्सदाशिवापरावतारमूर्ति–
चतुष्षष्टिकला विलास विहारमूर्ति–
बौद्धादिसर्ववादि दानवनृसिंहमूर्ति–
वर्णाश्रमवैदिक सिद्धांतोद्धारकमूर्ति–
मामकीनसाम्राज्य व्यवस्थापनमूर्ति–
विश्वेश्वर विश्वगुरु पद जगज्जेगीयमान मूर्ति–
निखिलयोगिचक्रवर्ति–

श्रीमच्छंकर भगवत्पादपादपद्मयोः

भ्रमणायमानस्य सुधन्वनो मम सोमवंश चूडामणि युधिष्ठिर पारंपर्यपरिप्राप्त भरतवर्षस्यांजलिबंधपूर्विकेयं राजन्यस्य विज्ञप्तिः ।।"

भगवद्भिर्दिग्विजयोऽकारि । सर्वेवादिनः पराजिताः ।

सर्वेवर्णा आश्रमाश्च कृतयुगवत्पूर्णवैदिकाध्वनि । नियोजितास्संतो यथाशास्त्र माचरतिहि धर्मं । ब्रह्म विष्णु महेश्वर महेश्वरीस्थानान्यशेषदेशवर्तीन्युध्धृतानि । सर्वंब्रह्मकुलमुद्धारितं । विशिष्यास्मद्राजन्यकुल मान्वीक्षिक्याद्यशेष राजतंत्र परिशीलनेन्नोन्नीतं भवति । ब्रह्मक्षत्राद्यस्मत्प्रमुख निखिल विनेयलोक संप्रार्थनया चतस्रोधर्मराजधान्यो, जगन्नाथ, बदरी, द्वारका, श्रृंगर्षिक्षेत्रेषु. भोगवर्धनज्योति श्शारदाश्रृंगेरी मठापर संज्ञिकाः संस्थापिताः । तत्रोत्तरदिशो योगिजनप्राधान्येन धर्म मर्यादारक्षणं सुकरमेवेति ज्योतिर्मठे श्री तोटकापरनाम्नो प्रतर्दनाचार्या । नथ श्रृंगेर्याश्रमे श्रृंगर्षि समस्वभावान् पृथ्वीधराभिधेय हस्तामलकाचार्यान । भोगवर्धने स्वतएवाभिमततत्वे नात्यंतोग्र स्वभावानपि सर्वज्ञकल्प पद्मपादापरनाम सनंदनाचार्या । नथ बौद्ध कापालकादि सकलवादि भूयिष्ठ पश्चिमस्यांदिशिवादिदैत्यांकुरः पुनर्माभवत्विति शारदापीठेखिल द्वारकायां जैनैरुत्सादित वज्रनाभनिर्मित भगवदालयादि दुर्दशां दूरीकृत्य, भगवद्भिः त्रिलोक सुंदरनाम्ना पुनस्सन्निबद्ध भगवदालय श्रीकृष्णादि सकल मर्यादा सुसंस्कृतायांमधिगताशेष लौकिक वैदिकतंत्र विश्व विख्यातकीर्ति सर्वज्ञानमयान् विश्वारूपापरनाम सुरेश्वराचार्यांश्चास्म त्सर्वलोका मतिपूर्वकमभिषिच्यैवं चतुर्म्य आचारेभ्य श्चतस्रोदिशआदिष्ठा भारतवर्षस्य । तएते तत्तत्पीठप्रणाढ्यानिजं निजमेवमंडलं गोपायंतो वैदिक मार्गं मुद्भासयंतु । सर्वेवयं तत्तन्मंडलस्था ब्रह्मक्षत्रादयस्तत्तन्मंडलस्यैवाचार्यस्याधिकारोधिकृता वर्तिष्यामहे च । महद्विनिर्णय प्रसक्तेतु सुरेश्वराचार्या एवोक्त लक्षणतः सर्वत्रैव व्यवस्थापका भवंतु भगवता मनुशासनाच्च ।

अस्मद्राज सत्तैव निरंतर गुरुसत्ताऽप्युक्त मर्यादयाजगत्यविचलं विचलतु । परिव्राजकोहि महाकुलीनत्व वैदुष्यादि विशिष्टाचार्य लक्षणै-रन्वितएव । श्री भगवत्पाद पीठानामधिकार मर्हंति नतु त्रिनिमयेनेत्येव मार्गेनियमबंधो भगवदाज्ञा रामवबुद्धस्समस्तै रधास्मदादि ब्रह्म क्षत्रादि वंशोद्भवैः परमप्रेम्णोत्तमांगे नाद्रियत । इत्येतांविज्ञप्ति मंगीकुर्वंतु भगवंत इति । स्वस्त्यस्तु लोकेभ्यः ॥"

युधिष्ठिरशके ౨౬౬౩ | सुधन्वा सार्वभौमः
आश्वियुज शुद्ध ౧౫ |

This inscription is dated the year 2663 on the Yudhishtira Saka. The same year the Journey on the earth of Sir Sankara came to a close. The Great Acharya lived only for 32 years- The years of his birth and demise therefore work out to 2631 and 2663 of the Yudhishtira Era or B. C. 509 and B. C. 477. The four great religious institutions known as the great Sankara Peethas were established by him as follows in the years noted ageinst each:-

At Dwaraka (Saradamutta) in B. C. 491.
At Badari (Jyotirmatha) in B. C. 486.
At Jagannadha or Puri in B. C. 485.
At Sringeri in B. C. 484.

These great religious institutions developed their own branches in turns and they have been in existence, under an unbroken of administrators. Of the subordinate branches of the Sringeri Peetha two have attained considerable vogue in this part (Andhra) of the country. Pushpagiri and Adhinava Virupaksha. (of which the author is the present incumbent). The lists of successive heads of these Peethas are all preserved in the respective Peethas and reckoning back with the help of these lists we can arrive at the time of the foundation of the Peethas. The copperplate inscription of Emperor Sudhanva proves that the year of the demise of Sri Sankara is 2663 of the Yudhishtira Era or B. C. 477-76. The beginning of the Yudhishtira Era is the time of the Maha_bharata War. It had already been proved to be B. C. 3138. So Sri Sankara's life works out to B. C. 509 to B. C. 477-476,. Yudhishtira Era 2662 + 476 = 3138 B. C.

Fifth: Other inscriptions :

1. In gift deeds dated on the Gupta Era Mahaabharata War is referred to (Vide Fleet C II, 120, 124, 129, 134, 139.)

2. An inscription found in the temple of Madhukeswara in the villege Banavasi in the North Canara district, is dated 168 of the Yudhishtira Era. It must have been inscribed in B. C. 3138 — 168 = B.C. 2970.

3. The inscriptions in the Belgaum District of the Mysore State are dated on the Yudhishtira Era. (Vide Journey of Dr. Fleet through Mysore, Canara, and Malabar -III pp 231, 411.)

* * * *

# AGE OF THE MAHABHARATA WAR

## TOPIC - IX.

### OPINIONS OF HISTORICAL SCHOLARS

1. Dr. Wilson writes :- The general fact (is) that the dynasties prior to Krishna precede the time of the Great War and the beginning of the Kali age, both which events are placed five thousand years ago, (Vide Wilson's Vishnupurana, London Edition P. P. LXIV and LXV).

2. The Kurupandava War was fought 37 years before Kali, that is 3139 B. C. (Vide History of Classical Sanskrit Literature by M. Krishnamachariar, Intro - XLIII).

3. Encyclopaedia Brittanica 14th edition 5th volume p. 658; "The Kaliyuga Era is the principal Astronomical Reckoning of the Hindus. It is frequently, if not generally, shown in the Almanacs............ Its initial point lay in 3102 B.C., and the year 5002 of Kali began in A. D. 1900".

4. The famous Mahammadan Astronomer Mr. Alberuni mentioned in his Indian History that 1031 A.D is equavalent to 4132 of Kali Era i. e. 3101 B. C., (Vide Alberuni's India, translated by Dr. E. C. Sachaun, IInd vol, 49th chapter 5-7 pages.)

5. Mr. Lionel, D. Barnett in his book 'Antiquities of India' Ed. 1913 published by Warner writes thus:

"The Kali Era is supposed to begin from 3102 B. C." (P. 94)

"The present Age, which is the Kaliyuga is reckoned as having begun in the year 3102 B. C. (page 193).

6. Prof : Buchanan mentions an inscription in the temple of Madhukeswara at, Banvasi in North Canara dated in the 168th year of Yudhishtira Era. (i. e., Yudhishtira Era begins With the year of the Mahabharata War 3138 B. C. – 168 = 2970 B. C.)

7. Prof. M. A. Trayer in his commentary on 'Rajatarangini' also admitted and adopted this Kali Era which started in B. C. 3102. Mr. C. V. Vaidya in his Epic History admitted that Kaliyuga 1 is equivalent to 3101. B. C.

8. The Nepala Rajavamsavali or the history of Nepal followed the same Kali Saka that started in 3102 B. C. (Vide Ind. Ant, Vol. XIII. P. 411 ff)

9. Dr. Buhler also admitted and adopted B. C. 3102 as the starting point of Kali Era and Kali 26 or 3076 B. C. as the starting Point of Loukika Era or the Saptarshi Era in his commentary on Nepal history and on the manuscript of Kashmir history (Rajatrangini). (Vide Indian Antiquary Vol V, 27th page ff. Ed. 1876)

* * * *

# AGE OF THE MAHABHARATA WAR

## TOPIC - X

## NO INSCRIPTIONAL EVIDENCE TO THE ANCIENT HISTORY OF BHARAT BY THE MODERN HISTORIANS

It is wrong, to claim that the history of ancient Bharat, of the Eupopean Orientalists and their disciples, is based on the evidence of inscriptions.

The Western Historians have claiming that they have based their histories of ancient Bharat on the evidence of available inscriptions. But it cannot be substantiated. The corner stone of the history of ancient Bharat, even for these European historians, is the date of the Mahabharata War. But they have not arrived at any clear determination of it even up to now. They have been indulging in mere varied conjectures that it might have occurred in the 24th, 19th, 15th, 14th, 11th, or 9th century before Christ. For the rest, they have no other reliable source for their histories of ancient Bharat except the 'Mahabharata' and the Puranas. Their only contribution to the history of ancient Bharat is the theory of the contemporaneity of Alexander, the Greek conqueror and Maurya Chandragupta, which is a baseless and wrong theory. They have no inscriptional or historical evidence to produce in favour of this theory. Indigenous historical literature, our purnas, indicate that Alexander's contemporary in

India was Chandra Gupta of the Gupta dynasty who was reigning in B. C. 327 and could not be Chandragupta of the Maurya dynasty of Magadha who belongs to B. C. 1534.

No evidence of any inscription has been adduced for their determinations of the dates of the birth and demise of the Buddha. They have made false propaganda that there is mention of the year 164 in the Kharavela inscription but there is no mention of the year 164 or any other year in that inscription. There is no inscriptional or historical evidence to assign the inscriptions of Asoka to B. C. 272-36; no date is any where mentioned or referred to in any of the inscription. There in no evidence or authority for the assumptions of these European Orientalists that the Yona Kings mentioned in the inscriptions are Greek princes or that Yona means Greek. There is no menton of the word 'Greek' in any of the inscriptions. There is no inscriptional evidence for the dates of the reigns of the different Kings of the various dynasties of Kings that ruled over the different parts of Bharat from the time of the Mahabharata War. The only authority for their accounts of all these reigns is our Puranas themselves. They are not aware of the Saka Era of B. C. 550 mentioned by Varahamihira, or the Sri Harsha Saka of B. C. 457 or the Malava Gana Saka of B. C. 725. They are not aware that the Gupta Era of B. C. 327 started with the reign of Chandragupta of the Gupta dynasty. They date it in A. D. 320 wrongly. Inspite of the vivid accounts of the historical personages of Vikramarka and Salivahana in our Puranas and in the indigenous histories of Kashmir, Nepal, and Magadha, they deny their historicity. There is no historical or inscriptional evidence in support of their pet theories or to confirm the writings of Ptolemy, Megasthenese and Heuntsang, by which they set so much stare. They have no ancient inscription to show of any century prior to the Christian Era. So it is preposterous to propagate as they have been doing, that their histories of ancient Bharat have been based on the evidence of inscriptions. There is a strong belief among the scholars of the traditional type, in our country, that such ancient inscriptions, were destroyed deliberately, as soon as they were discovered, because they disproved their theories and false histories. There is no limit to the outrages perpetrated by them to reduce the antiquity of the history of ancient Bharat. If no inscription of any of the centuries before Christ was discovered, how could their histories of ancient Bharat of the Centuries before Christ be besed on the evidence of inscriptions?

To know either the Bharata Yuddhakala or the Hindu dynasties and the periods for which they ruled, there is no other source than the Mahabharata, the Puranas and the Inscriptions shown in this book. They proved that Bharata Yuddhakala was 36 years before Kali or 3138 B. C. and listed out the various Hindu Dynasties that ruled continuously from the Mahabharata War 3138 B.C. to the twelth century after Christ.

# AGE OF THE MAHABHARATA WAR

## TOPIC - XI

### MOVEMENT OF THE SAPTARSHI MANDALA AND CONTEMPORARY OF ALEXANDER EXPLAINED

The Kali age began in B. C. 3102. The Mahabharata War occurred in B. C. 3138. The same year Parikshit was born; and the Yudhishtira Era was founded. 75 years befor Kali the Constellation of the Seven Sages entered the region of the star Magha. The Constellation remains in each star region for a hundred years before passing over into the next star region. The authors of our Puranas, and our Astronomers have, by their references to the positisn of the Constellation of the Seven Sages in relation to the reigns of the kings that ruled over the country managed to preventive as well as a corrective to any discrepancy that may otherwise creep into their accounts of the reigns of the kings. The European Oreintalists were in the beginning' unaware of the significance of this feature of the chronological references in our Puranas and consequently neglected and ignored it. But lateron they discovered that this was an unerring and indisputable authoritative instrument for detecting the erroneous chronological determinations propagated by them in their arbitrary historical writings with a view to deliberately reduce the antiquity of the history of ancient Bharat. They could not pooh pooh it. It is a natural measure and means of reckoning time.

It is based on science and can be verified by precise calculations. Mr. Pargiter was the first of the Modern Oreintalists of the Western schoal who attempted to find fault with it and justify their erroneous chronological determinations. But he has only exposed himself to ridicule by his outrageous attempt. Still his false theories and erroneous conclusions are deemed authoritative by our modern historians. They have not been able to detect the mischief of which he was guilty. It is shown below.

The connection between the basic facts of the history of ancient Bharat and the movement of the Constellation of the Seven sages is established in the verses given below 38, 39, 40, 41, and 47 of chapter 271 of the Matsya Purana.

श्लो ॥ महापद्माभिषेकात्तु यावज्जन्म परीक्षितः ।
एकमेव सहस्रं तु ज्ञेयं पंचशतोत्तरं ॥ – (मत्स्य-271-38)

" पौलोमास्तु तथांध्रास्तु महा पद्मांतरे पुनः ।
अनंतरं शतान्यष्टौ षट्त्रिंशत् तु समास्तथा ॥ ("- 271-39)

" तावत्कालांतरंभाव्य मांध्रांतादा परीक्षितः ।
भविष्येते प्रसंख्याताः पुराणज्ञैः श्रुतर्षिभिः ॥ ("- 271-40)

" सप्तर्षयस्तदाप्राहुः प्रदीप्ते नाग्निना समाः ।
सप्तविंशति भाव्यानां मांध्राणांतु यथापुनः ॥ ("- 271-41)

" ब्राह्मणास्तु चतुर्विंशा भविष्यंति शतंसमाः ।
ततः प्रभृत्ययं सर्वलोकोव्यापत्स्यते भृशं ॥ ("- 271-47)

They mean :- From the time of birth of Parikshit i. e., the time of the Mahabharata War to the time of the coronation of Mahapadma nanda, king of Magadha, it should be known that 1500 years passed. (38)

In the same manner from the time of Mahapadmananda to the time of the Andhras who were Poulomas, in addition to the 1500, another 836 years passed. (39) -

From the time of Parikshit to the time with the Andhras at the end, the interval is to be reckoned 1500+836 or 2336 years, according to the Sages well versed in Puranas. (40)

(The expression 'Andhrantaat' in the above verse-40 is gramatically capable of two interpretations- one taking it as a Bahuvrihi samasa- 'is the time with the Andhras at the end or the time up to the advent of the Andhras' or taking it as Shasti Tatpurusha- 'as the time of the fall of the distruction of the Andhras or to the end of the reigns of the Andhras.' But obviously the verse proposes to fix the times of the kings and not to foretell the destruction of any dynasty. It is clear by the next verse 41).

By the time of the birth of Parikshit, the Seven Sages were in the star Krittika associated with the fire God Agni. In the time of the same Andhras, after completing a cycle of 27 stars in 2700 years, they will be once again in in the same star Krittika and the cycle repeats itself. (271 - 41).

By the time of the 24th king of the Andhra dynasty Siva Satakarni, in Yudhishtira Saka 2705, they were in Krittika again, and the cycle repeats itself. The other Andhra kings (from the 25th to the 32nd) ruled for 106 years. So by the end of the Andhra dynasty from the time of the Mahabharnta War or the birth of Parikshit in B. C. 3138, (2705 + 106) or 2811 years passed. That is, the Andhra dynasty came to a close in B. C. (3138 - 2811) = 327 B. C. That was the beginning of the Gupta dynasty of Magadha. Alexander's invasion of India is dated 326 B. C. So his contemporary in India could only be Chandra gupta of the Gupta dynasty and not Chandragupta of the Maurya dynasty.

A careful study of the movement of the Contellation of the Seven Sages also proves the truth of the fact.

When the Seven Sages are in the 24th star century the land will be subject to many evils. (Matsys 271 - 47).

Verse 423 of chapter 99 of the Vayupurana states it more clearly thus:

श्लो ।। सप्तर्षियोमघायुक्ताः कालेपारिक्षित्ते गतं ।
आंध्रांशे सचतुर्विंशे भविष्यंति मतेमम ।। (वायु ९९-४२३)

which means: At the time of the birth of Parikshit (ie. the time of the Mahabharata War the Seven Sages were in Magha. By the time of the Andhras (the beginning of the rule of the Andhra dynasty) they reach the 24th star century.

| | |
|---|---|
| From the birth of Parikshit to the coronation of Mahapadma nanda 1500 years; but (if we add up the figures given for the reigns of the individual kings in the list in the Puranas it works out to). .... | 1504 |
| From Mahapadma nanda to the beginning of the Andhra dynasty. | 801 |
| | 2305 |

That is, after the birth of Parikshit, in the 24th cetury the rule of the Andhra dynasty commences. By the time of 35th year of the Andhra rule, 2340 years pass since the Mahabharata War. Thereafter the length of the reigns of the Andhra Princes 460 years (2340 + 460 =) 2800 years on the whole.

The difference of eleven years is due to slight discrepancies in reckoning the reigns of the individual kings. If we add 11, we get 2811 years from the time of the Mahabharata War to tho end of the Andhra dynasty. According to the Vayupurana also it is 2811 years. The movement of the Constellation of the Seven Sages therefore provided the authors of our Puranas with a valuable devise to correct slight discrepancies and indicates the broad intervals of time correctly.

The European historians of ancient Bharat identifying the Chandragupta known to have been the contemporary of Alexander in India in B. C. 326 as Maurya Chandra-gupta, deliberately ignoring even the obvious possibility of his being the Gupta-Chandragupta, managed to reduce the antiquity of the history of ancient Bharat by 12 centuries at one stroke. Similarly and in pursuance there of, Mr. Pargiter has tried to discover some discrepancies in the references in our Puranas to the movement of the Constellation of the Seven Sages and to push forward the date of the Mahabharata War from B. C. 3138., by several centuries. The mischief perpetrated by Mr. Pargiter is exposed here below :—

## Mr. Pargiter's "Dynasties of the Kali Age".

According to the historical accounts in the Puranas and the references to the movement of the Constellation of the Seven Sages the time of the Mahabharata War is fixed at 36 years before Kali or 3138 B. C. Mr. Pargiter alleges that the verse in the Purana is incorrect, and amends it deliberately to suit his own preconceived notions and calcultions. But his emendation does not carry conviction, on the other hand it proves rediculous. In his dynasties of the Kali Age, he quotes on page 59, the verse 271-41 of the Matsya Purana which gives the movement of the Seven Sages, after completing the cycle of 27 stars in 2700 years in the time of the same Andhra Kings. It means from the time of the Mahabharata War in B. C. 3138, up to the time of the 24th prince of the Andhra royal dynasty the Seven Sages will move round the 27 stars in 27 centuries and come back to the same position. According to the Puranas by the end of the reign of the 24th king of the Andhra dynasty 2705 elapsed since the Mahabharata War. The reigns of the remaining eight kings of the Andhra dynasty from the 25th to the 32nd together make up 106 years. So by the end of the Andhra dynasty, the time that elapsed since the Mahabharata War works out to 2811 years. Mr. Pargiter alleges that the verse 271 - 41 of Matsya Purana is incorrect and emends it to suit his convenience.

The first line of Matsya 271-41 reads:

"सप्तर्षयस्तदाप्राहुः प्रदीप्तेनाग्निना समाः।"

The same sentence is found in the Vayu and Brahmanda Puranas with a slight variation :-

"सप्तर्षयस्तदाप्राहुः प्रदीप्तेराग्नि वै शतं।"

which means: At that time (of the birth of Parikshit in 3138 B.C. the Seven Sages were in the star century of Krittika (associated with the God Agni). Then the second line reads the same without any variation, in all the Puranas.

"सप्तविंशति भाव्यानामांध्राणांतु यथापुनः॥"

"After 2700 years, they will be again in the same star in the same Andhra period". (The Reader may be puzzled to find it stated that the Seven Sages were in Magha in Vayu 99-423 and in

Krittika in Matsya 271-41) at some other places in the Puranas at the same time. But the seeming inconsistency can be easily explained. The Constellation of Seven Sages is a long Constellation of Seven stars in a zigzag line. It is possible that in the course of its movement at any one time, if the star of the Constellation at one end is in one star, the star at the other end may be in another star and these who observe the position of the Constellation may note it with reference to the star at the one end or the star at the other end throughout consistently. Then there will be no difference in the intervals of time measured by the movement of the Constellation. A detailed account regarding the movement of this Constellation is given by Alexander Cunningham under the caption 'Saptarshi Era' on page 17 of his Indian Eras, with the help of a table which is reproduced at the end of Chapter VI of this volume.

The above verse 271-41 of the Mastya Purana has been emended by Mr. Pargiter to suit his intention to reduce the time of the antiquity of the Mahabharata War thus. His emended version reads :-

"सप्तर्षयस्तदापुष्ये प्रतीपेराज्ञिवै समं ।"

(Vide page 75 and foot-note 4 on page 59 of his Kali Age). Which means: "Then, while Pratipa was reigning, the Seven Sages were in the star Pushyami". The reason he alleges for emending the text of the Puranas is simply that the text of the Purana seemed to him to be wrong. But really there is nothing wrong with the text in the purana. He then explains the meaning of the verse as emended by him "The Great Bear was situated equally with regard to the lunar Constellation Pushyami while Pratipa was king. At the end of the Andhras who will be in the 27th century afterwards, the cyclo repeats itself."

"The Great Bear was conjoined with Magha in Parikshit's time for 100 years. It will be in (ie. Conjoined with) the 24th Constellation for 100 years at the termination of the Andhras" (Dynasties of the Kali Age page 75).

Foot - Note 4: "This statement read with the preceding statements would imply that some 814 years are allowed for the interval between Pratipa and Parikshit. Thus Pratipa to Parikshit 814 years. Parikshit to Mahapadma Nanda 1050 years, Mahapadmananada to the last Andhra king 836 years, total 2700 years".

The Great Bear being in Pushyami, Pratipa reigning at that time, the interval from Pratipa to Parikshit being 814 years — — all these statements are entirely the concoction, inconsistent and obsurd of Mr. Pargiter and do not find a place anywhere in any Purana. Thus, with the help of his own unwarrented emendation of the verse in the Puranas Mr. Pargiter arrives at (2700 – 814) = 1886 years for the interval from the Mahabharata War to the end of the Andhra dynasty. The expression, in the Purana means only at the time of the Andhras and not at all 'at the termination of the Andhras'. Mr. Pargiter is obviously wrong in stating that the Great Bear took 814 years to move from Pushyami to Magha, a distance of only two stars in two hundred years.

The Modern history of ancient Bharat by European Orientalists and their Indian disciples is full of such atrocities deliberately perpetrated to mislead the people of Bharat and prevent them from ever knowing their real history. Countless such atrocities can be proved against Dr. Buhler in the histories of Kashmir and Nepal. The sentences in the footnote 4 by Mr. Pargiter can mislead only such students of Bharat as are not acquainted with Sanskrit. He says "This statement read with the preceding statements would imply that some 814 years are allowed for the interval between Pratipa and Parikshit." But in the preceding verses referred to there is no expression which could mean 814 years, no mention of any Pratipa, or of the star Pushyami. It is all the concoction of his brain.

Let us concede, as Mr. Pargiter alleges that 10 Kings reigned from Pratipa to Parikshit at the time of the Mahabharata War. The total period covered by their 10 reigns is according to him 814 years. In his criticism of the Chronological details in the Puranas, earlier in his volume 'Kali Age' he opines that a period of 1000 years assigned for the reigns of 32 kings is excessive, and a period of 723 years for 16 kings is absurd and therefore the statements in the Puranas with regard to time are unreliable. (Vide page 13 of his Kali Age.)

How can he himself now suggest for the reigns of ten kings 814 years which works out at 81½ years per reign?

He has not hesitated further to allot 814 years for the movement of the Great Bear from Pushyami to Magha a distance of two stars in the face of the recognised astronomical fact that the Great Bear takes one hundred years to move from one star to the next and two hundred years to move from Pushyami to Aslesha and then to Magha.

* * * *

# AGE OF THE MAHABHARATA WAR

## TOPIC - XII

### FALSE PROPAGANDA OF THE EUROPEAN ORIENTALISTS

That the Kali Yuga began in B.C. 3102 on the 20th of February at 2-27' -30" hours was known to all the European Orientalists from Sir William Jones who laid the foundations for the history of ancient Bharat in 1774 to Vincent A. Smith of 1915. They knew also the Mahabharata War took place 36 years before Kali or in 3138 B.C. But they do not admit it openly. Still it is undeniable that it was known to them. Dr. Wilson disclosed to his European friends in 1825 that the Saptarshi Era began in Kali 26. So all the three Eras dating from the Mahabharata War and the victory of Yudhishtira the Niryana of Sri Krishna and the advent of Kali and the Swargarohana of Yudhishtira and the passing of the Seven Sages from Magha into the next star were all well-known to the European Orientalists, but, with the deliberate and intention of bringing forward the date of the Mahabharata War for reducing the antiquity of the history of ancient Bharat and to discredit the historical value of our Puranas, they do not profess the knowledge but appear to be ignorant of them. (Vide Vol. IV of Jone's Works p.52

of the 1778 Edn., 'On The Chronology of the Hindus' .... "The year 4891 Kali corresponds to 1790 of the Christian Era.")

The later Orientalists were also aware of the commencement of the Kali Era in 3102 B. C. But they have been consistently declaring all through that for the reconstruction of the chronology of the history of ancient Bharat there was no welknown event of definite date previous to the invasion of Alexander and therefore they were obliged to start with the identification of the contemporary of Alexander in India at the time of his invasion in B. C. 326-324 and managed to identify Chandragupta of the Maurya Dynasty who really belongs to B. C. 1534 as the contemporary of Alexander in B. C., 324. Really the contemporary of Alexander was Chandragupta of the Gupta dynasty. So their false propaganda began with the statement of "No date or public event can be fixed before the invasion of Alexander", of Elphinstone (Vide his History of India p. 11 in fifth Edition). Next Max-Muller also declared similarly. (Vide pp. 3-8 of the 1859 edition of his History of Ancient Sanskrit Literature and the same statement is repeated in Dr. Fleet's article on 'Epigraphy in the Indian Empire' Imperial Gazetteer of India, Vol. II. pp. 3-6).

By such repeated false propaganda they have been able to mislead all studets of ancient Indian history and by dating Chandragupta Maurya of 1534 B. C. in B. C. 324, to reduce the antiquity of Ancient Indian History at the very beginning by 1534 – 324 = 1210 years.

Sir William Jones himself has recorded that he knew that according to the Puranas the invasion of Alexander occurred after the reigns of the Satavahana kings of the Andhra dynasty. He has also stated his opinion that the end of the reign of the Andhra dynasty was in 452 B.C., obviously he was aware that Alexander invaded India in B. C., 326. In these circumstances to base the chronology of the history of ancient Bharat on the invasion of India of Alexander which does not find any place in any of our Puranas could only be the result of a deliberate intention to reduce the antiquity of our history and culture. (Vide Jone's works Vol. IV- on the Chronology of the Hindus.)

* * * *

# AGE OF THE MAHABHARATA WAR

## TOPIC - XIII.

### HISTORY OF MAGADHA
### OR HISTORY OF MODERN ANCIENT INDIA

Of all the countries in the world Bharat has the most ancient history and culture. To reduce the antiquity of its history and culture first the Christian Missionaries and then the so called Orientalists, deliberately conspired and plotted. The French savant Louise Jaccoliot writes in his 'Bible-le-Indi' "The Reverend Fathers, Jesuits, Fransicians, Sranger Missions and other corporations unite with touching harmony in India to accomplish a work of Vendalism, which it is right to denounce as well to the learned world as to Orientalists. Every manuscript, every Sanskrit work that falls into their hands is immediately condemned and consigned to the flames. Needless to say that the choice of these gentlemen always falls from preference upon those of the highest antiquity, and whose authenticity may appear incontestable". ................

"Every new arrival receives a formal order so to dispose of all that may fall into his hands. Happily, happily, the Brahmins do not open to them the secret stores of their literary wealth, Philosophic and religious." (Vide Louise Jaccoliot's Bible-le-Indi and Mr. N. Chidambara Iyyer's Varahamihira's Brihat Samhita — — English Translation, Introduction p.2 foot note)

Sumitra, king of Ayodhya, of the Ikshvaku dynasty and Kshemaka, king of Hastinapura both passed away childless in Kali 1504 or B. C., 1634. So the Kingdom of Magadha gained ascendancy and the kings of Magadha became the Emperors of Bharat. The history of Magadha is thus narrated in the Puranas:

श्लो ॥ "संग्रामे भारते वृत्ते सहदेवे निपातिते ।
सोमाधि स्तस्य दायादो राजाभूत्सगिरिव्रजे ॥"

" "पंचाशतं तताष्टौच समा राज्य मकारयत् ॥
श्रुतश्रवाश्चतुष्षष्टि समास्तस्यान्वयेभवत् ॥"

When Sahadeva (son of Jarasandha and king of Magadha) was killed in the Mahabharata War his cousin Somadhi (alias Somapi) was crowned at Girivraja, capital of Magadha. He ruled over Magadha for 58 years. His son Srutasrava ruled for 64 years after him. Thus they (the Puranas) proceed to mention 22 kings and the periods of their reigns and then it is stated that these 22 kings of the dynasty ruled in all for 1000 years on the whole. But when we total up the figures for the individual reigns of the 22 kings, after collating the accounts in the various Puranas, and add them up, the total works out to 1006 years. The difference of 6 years is comparatively insignificant. Thus according to similar carefully worded and consistent accounts in the Puranas.

| | |
|---|---|
| 22 kings of the Barhadradha dynasty ruled for | 1006 years |
| after that 5 kings of Pradyota dynasty ruled for | 138 years |
| after that 10 kings of the Sisunaga dynasty ruled for | 360 years |
| after that 2 kings of the Nanda dynasty ruled for | 100 years |
| | 1604 years |

It was then, after the Nandas, that Chandragupta - Maurya became the king of Magadha. His time therefore works out to the time of the Mahabharata War B. C. 3138 – 1604 = 1534 B. C. But the European Orientalists pretend ignorance of the Kali Era or the time of the Mahabharata War, introduce the date 324 B. C., of Alexander's invasion of India, and pretending to identify Chandragupta founder of the Maurya dynasty as the contemporary of Alexander in India, fix the date of Chandragupta Maurya at B. C. 324. Thus they have managed to reduce the antiquity of the ancient history of Bharat and push forward its entire chronology by 1534-324 = 1210 years. In consequence of this initial mischief the date of every well - known event in the history of Bharat is rendered doubtful and a subject of controversy. The turth is the contemporary of Alexander was not Chandragupta of the Maurya dynasty but Chandragupta of the Gupta Dynasty.

If we correctly identify the contemporary of Alexander as Chandragupta of the Gupta dynasty and reckoning the periods of reigns of the kings of the several royal dynasties of Magadha as given in Puranas, proceed backwards, the time of the Mahabharata War works out correctly to B. C. 3138. So if this fundamental error in the identification of the contemporary in India of Alexander the Great, be rectified we can arrive at a correct chronology for the entire history of ancient Bharat. Such a chronology is available in the previous publications of this author 'Ancient Hindu History Parts I and II."

There is no evidence of inscriptions or coins or reliable history for this theory of the contemporaneity of Alexander the Great and Chandragupta of the Maurya dynasty of Magadha advanced as proved fact by these European Orientalists and their disciples. The independent evidence they are able to cite in support of their theory, is the reference in the writings of a Chinese pilgrim who visited India thousands of years after Maurya Chandragupta, evidently based on the information he was able to gather from his chance companions on the way with his cursory acquaintance with their language. These references of a foreign trveller based on hearsay are held as authoritative evidence for the history of ancient Bharat. But the writings of Sri Veda

Vyasa, regarded by the people of Bharat as a very incarnation of God, who was an eye witness to the Mahabharata War and reduced what he actually saw to writing in the great National Epic of India, the Mahabharata and the other Puranas, revered as sacred religious treatises throughout the country all these centuries down to the present time, are rejected by these European Orientalists as unreliable and invalid as evidence for history. In the law of no country do we find any the best importance attached to hearsay evidence. But it is such hearsay evidence that is held as the supreme authority for the ancient history of Bharat. The European Orientalists and their superstitious followers among Indian historians and students and professors of history are now filled with such reverence for the modern false history af ancient Bharat whose foundation are based on such flimsy evidence, that they are not prepared to consider the evidence of inscriptions, if it goes against the false and erroneous determinations of their history.

* * * *

# AGE OF THE MAHABHARATA WAR

## TOPIC - XIV.

### HISTORY OF KASHMIR

Kalhana, a scholar and son of a Chief Minister of the State of Kashmir, wrote a history of Kashmir in the Sanskrit language. In the introductory verses he describes the procedure and principles followed by him in writing his history.

श्लो ।। पूर्वैर्बद्धं कथावस्तु मयि भूयोनिबध्नति ।
प्रयोजनमनाकर्ण्य वैमुख्यं नोचितंसतां ।। (राज तरंगिणि 1.8)

" दृष्टं दृष्टं नृपोदंतं बध्वाप्रमयमीयुषाम् ।
अवक्काल भवैंवर्तियितप्रबंधेषु पूर्यते ।। ( " " 1.9)

" दाक्ष्यकियदिदं तस्मादस्मिन्भूतार्थवर्णने ।
सर्वप्रकारंस्खलिते योजनाय मयोद्यमः ।। ( " " 1.10)

Which means: "I am rewriting the history previously written by the ancients (earier writers); but (on that account) it should not be ignored or neglected without noting the purpose (it is intended to serve). The histories of the ancient kings were recorded each by scholars contemporary to the king, and eye-witnesses with first hand know. ledge of the events of the kings reign. They wrote them in seperate volumes and made their exit from this world. But the historians of recent times compiled those records of eyewitnesses into continuous treatises, but included in them rumours and beliefs current in their times and anecdotes gathered by them from hearsay. By the incorporation of such hearsay matter, several inconsistencies and mutual contradictions arose in their histories. In doing so there is neither dexterity nor intellect. Therefore, in writing this ancient history, my main purpose is to remedy such errors and correct these contradictions, with the help of old records, gift deeds, inscriptions etc., that are at my disposal. Several scholars such as Suvrata, Chavillakara, and others had attempted before me. There are eleven such histories by previous scholars. I have studied carefully these eleven histories, and in addition the Neela Purana by Neela Muni, the inscriptions of the ancient kings, the learned (scientific) treatises produced in their times, the songs of the court poets in which the qualities and achievements of the kings were celebrated, and I am, with this eqipment, endeavouring in this volume, to produce a true correct history of Kashmir."

Thus Kalhana prefaces his history in the 8th, 9th and 10th verses of the 1st chapter of his Rajatarangini. He never meddled with the lists of the kings of the periods of their reigns. He has simply eschewed the hearsay matter incorporated by later writers with the authentic records of the original writers who were eyewitnesses with first hand knowledge of what they wrote about. Evidently he held that hearsay information cannot be valid matter for history.

The histories of India prepared by the European Orientalists are all mainly based on such hearsay evidence held to be the most valid authority for historical purposes. These European Orientalists have further rejected as invalid and unauthorative the indigenous historical writings in our epic 'The Mahabharata' and the Puranas etc., written by eye witnesses like Veda Vyasa. On the same principle they have rejected the Rajatarangini of Kalhana as a historical document of questionable validity. Alleging that he deviated in places from the earlier histories on which he based his history, they have altogether rejected, the first three Tarangas or chapters of his Rajatarangini, and interpolating and emending his text in several places in the subsequent Tarangas, to suit the determinations of their own histories based on fantastic theories and hearsay evidence, managed to reduce the antiquity of the history of Kashmir, as they did similarly, with regard to the history of Magadha, by 1200 years. The process by which they manoeuvred this nefarious achievement is given below.

According to the history of Kashmir, the king who was on the throne about the time of the Mahabharata War, Gonanda I, was related to Jarasandha king of Magadha. He had joined his relation Jarasandha in the latter attack on Sri Krishna and seize of Madhura, and taking part in the battle with his armies, died on the battle field there, at the hands of Balarama. His son Damodara I who succeeded him to the throne of Kashmir attended the Swayamavara or function arranged for the choice of husband by the daughter of the king of Gandhara, attempted to interfere with the programme and was therefore killed there by Sri Krishna himself. Then Lord Sri Krishna proceeded to Kashmir and clearing the doubts of the ministers of the state who were hesitating to place a woman on the throne, arranged for the crowning of Damodara's wife who was then carrying. In a faw months the queen gave birth to a male child who was named as Gonanda II, and the ministers placed the child on the throne and crowned him (Gonanda II). It was only a short time thereafter that the Mahabharata War occurred. But as the king of Kashmir was a minor, neither of the contesting parties, the Kauravas and the Pandavas, sought his help, according to our history. He was then only a child of two in B. C., 3138. So he must have been born in B. C. 3140. According to Kalhana, the coronation of Gonanda III, a later king of the same dynasty, was celebrated 2330 years before the time of Kalhana himself, who was writing in 1148 A. D., ie. in (2330 - 1148) = 1182 B. C. The 12th king after him (Gonanda III of the same dynasty was Mihira Kula. He was a true Kshatriya. He belonged to B. C. 704 to B. C. 634. The European Orientalists hold that Toramana, a prince of the eighteenth generation among his (Mihirakula's) descendents who really belonged to B. C. 16, was the father of Mihirakula and that this Toramana was a Huna (a foreigner - non Indian) and profess that they are unaware of the region from which these Hunas came over to India, or their previous history or dynasty. These are obviously fantastic fictions and absolutely false stories. Their attempt is to push forward this (alleged) foreign king af Kashmir 'Mihirakula' from B.C. 704-634 to A.D. 632 ie., by 13 centuries and taking this date of Mihirakula as the corner store for the chronology of the history of Kashmir, as their date 324 B.C. for Chandragupta Maurya for the chronology of the history of Magadha, and thus reduce the antiquity of the entire history of Kashmir and ancient Bharat by 12 or 13 centuries, on the whole.

In support of this theory of theirs they refer to the inscriptions nos, 164, 165 of Mandasar. But there is no date in either of them. And they are spurious, manoeuvred by them to justify their fantastic assumptions (Vide History of Kashmir by this Author). Here is the true story or Toramana. The king of Kashmir, of the 17th generation among his descendents, of Mihirakula who was a genuine Bharatiya and Kshatriya was Pravara-Sena. He had two sons by name Hiranya and Toramana, princes of the 18th generation after Mihirakula of the royal dyansty of Kashmir. In time, on the death of Pravarasena Hiranya the elder of the two became the king. Toramana functioned as Yuvaraja or Crown prince and attended to part of the task of the administration of the kingdom. For gererations, the image of a female deity 'Baala' had been inscribed on the coins of the realm. 'Baala' was the special chosen deity of the royal family of Kashmir. Toramana withdrew from circulation the coins bearing the image of the diety 'Baala' and reminted them with his own image instead and introduced the new coins into the currency. The king came to know of this freak, indulged in by the Crown-prince without his sanction took offence and objection to the innovation and put Toramana in prison. The wife of Toramana was also living with the prince, with the permission of the king. In course of time she was confined and for the confinement she was sent by Toramana secretly to a potter in whom he had especial confidence. There, in the pottor's house, the princes was delivered of a male child who was named after his grandfather, 'Pravara - Sena II'. Toramana later died in the prison. King Hiranya also died childless in A. D. 14. Mean-while Pravarasena II, the son of Toramana had started with his mother on a tour to the sacred places of pilgrimage. So there was no king on the throne or a suitable prince with any claim to be placed on the throne. Vikramaditya king of Ujjain had established himself the acknowledged Emperor of Bharat by that time. To avoid the danger of anarchy, the ministers of the kingdom of Kashmir sent up a petition to him to nominate suitable ruler for their state. "Emperor Vikramaditya" nominated Mathrugupta, a distinguished poet in his court, also known for his administrative talent, and sent him to rule over Kashmir in A. D. 14. This is the detailed account of the episode of Toramana in the first 3 Tarangas of Kalhana's History of Kashmir.

This part of history, as the other parts, was evidently based on valid sources, as professed by Kalhana in the prefatory verses I- 8, 9, 10 of Kalhana, describing the principles and procedure he chose to adopt for his history. From the account in Kalhana's history, Hiranya and Toramana jointly administered the country, Kashmir, from B. C. 16 to A. D. 14. Vikramarka nominated a king for Kashmir, in his capacity as suzerain, being the Emperor of Bharat. Mihirakula and Toramana were both Kshatriyas and princes of the royal family of Kashmir. Vikramaditya was Emperor of Bharat. Alleging that Kalhana tampered with his authorities in these portions the Europan Orientalists have rejected just these three Tarangas, which contain such important historical facts, as invalid for historical purposes. They profess to write the history of Kashmir relying on Kalhana's text from the 4th Taranga onwards. They have been indulging in the false propaganda that Vikramarka of the 1st century A. D., is not a historical personage at all, and the Saka named after him was not founded by any such Emperor. This mischief has not yet been discovered by our Indian historians. Mihirakula and Toramana were Kshatriya princes of Kashmir in Bharat. They were not Hunas or foreigners. Hunas never ruled over any part of Bharat. Vikramaditya ruled as Emperor of Bharat from B. C. 82 to A. D. 19. The history of Kashmir concocted by Dr. Buhler and Stein is a heap of falsehoods and miserepresentations. We have to discard them and for a true history of Kashmir, rely entirely on Kalhana duly edited.

## The Story of the coins with the image of Toramana

'Emperor Vikramaditya' who had nominated Matrugupta as the king of Kashmir, passed away at the ripe old age of 120 years in A. D., 19 at

Ujjain. Filled with grief at the demise of his friend and patron, Matrugupta renounced the throne of Kashmir, took holy orders, went to Benaras and died there. By this time Pravarasena II son of Toramana had returned to Kashmir, with his mother, after completing the tour of pilgrimage to all the sacred shrines in the country. The ministers of the state therefore crowned him king at once and he proved a very able monarch. He even conquered the whole of the Indo-gangetic valley, central India and western India and ruled as a mighty king over all the regions, according to Kalhana. Throughout the vast dominions over which he exercised power, the coins bearing the image of his father were current. So as they were current coin in use in Western and Central India many of them have been discovered in the regions in modern times. But Mihirakula and Toramana were not Hunas, no Huna ever ruled over this part of India. The hearsay reports that a Chinese traveller in India in the 7th century A. D., had met Mihirakula could not be true. How could the Chinese traveller of the 7th century A. D. meet Mihirakula who belonged to 704-634 B. C? Such false statements must have been deliberately interpolated by Dr. Beal and other European Orientalists, in the Chinese manuscripts with the intention of gaining support for their false history of ancient Bharat. That is why, they have been carrying on incessent propaganda that the indigenous historical writings like the Puranas, Kashmir and Nepal histories etc., were not reliable and the accounts of foreign travellers have to be treated as authoritative evidence for the history of ancient

Bharat. But the statements alleged to be found in the writings of foreigners, which contradict the statements in our indigenous historical writings like histories of Kashmir and Nepal, Magadha, Epics and the Puranas, should be taken for recent interpolations and rejected and not held authoritative evidence.

* * * *

# AGE OF THE MAHABHARATA WAR

## TOPIC - XV.

## HISTORY OF NEPAL

### Confusion of the Eras ; Misinterpretations of inscriptions

Among the Royal dynasties of Nepal, the fifth was a Solar Dynasty. There are 31 kings in the list of Kings of this dyntsty. Of them the 27th is Sivadeva Varma. It is stated in the History of Nepal that this Sivadeva Varma was corwned king in Kali 2764. Three inscriptions of his have been discovered Nos. 12, 13, 14 of the Nepal inscriptions. In the inscription No 12, the coronation of Sivadeva Varma is dated the year 119 of the Sri Harsha Era (of 457 B. C) Kali 2764 or Sri Harsha 119 corresponds to B. C. 338. There is thus agreement with regard to this date between the history of Nepal and this inscription. But the European Orientalists, alleging that the date on the Kali Era in the history of Nepal is wrong, and that the Sri Harsha Saka (B.C. 457) of the inscription is a supposed Sri Harsha Siladitya Era commencing in A. D. 606, assign the coronation of Sivadeva Varma to A. D. 606 + 119 = A. D. 725, and thus by bringing forward the coronation of Sivadeva Varma from B.C. 338 to A.D. 725, reduce the antiquity of the entire history of Nepal by **1063 years,** and by further reducing the periods of the reigns of the kings wherever possible, on the whole reduce the antiquity of the Chronology of the history of Nepal, as they did with the Chronology of the history of Kashmir and Magadha by 1200 years.

The last king of the Solar dynasty is Viswadeva Varma. He ruled over Nepal from Kali 2950 to 3001. He had no male issue. He gave his only daughter in marriage to Amsumantha of the Thakore dynasty who succeeded Viswadeva Varma to the throne of Nepal and ruled over the country from Kali 3001 to 3069 or B. C. 101 - 33 B. C. He belongs to the sixth dynasty, (the Thakore dynasty) and the sixth king after Sivadeva Varma who was crowned in B. C. 338 and he was crowned 237 years subsequently in B. C. 101. During his reign, in Kali 3045 or B. C. 57, according to the Nepala Raja Vamsavali, or indigenous history of Nepal, Emperor Vikramaditya of Ujjain visited Nepal, and founded the Vikrama Era in 58-57 B. C., and the inauguration of the new Era was celebrated there. (Vide Indian Antiquary Vol. XIII P. 411 ff).

But Dr. Buhler, one of the European Orientalists who hold that there was no such Emperor Vikramaditya, he is only fictitious and not a historical personage, in order to ignore the reference to the visit of Vikramaditya to Nepal in the history of Nepal, introduces an account of the Chinese traveller in this connection and alleges that he learnt in response to an enquiry made by him, from his friend Dr. Beal who had made a study of the Chinese language and the Chinese manuscripts, that according to the Chinese manscripts of the record of the travels in India of

Heuntsang he visited Nepal in A. D. 637, and that he was then told there that at the very time or a short time previously there was a powerful king there of the name Amsumantha or 'Amshufamo' in Chinese of the manuscript. He therefore infers the Amsumanta, King of Nepal must have probably passed away a little previous to the visit of Heuntsang in A. D. 637 or just at the time, and we may date the time of Amsumanta in A. D. 637 and describes the statement in the Nepala Raja Vamsavali that Amsumantha was crowned in 101 B. C. as a false statement due to a desire on the part of the author of the work to increase the antiquity of the history of his country. Thus he manoeuvred (Dr. Buhler) to push forward the time of king Amsumantha of B. C. 101 to A. D. 637, and denies the historicity of Emperor Vikramaditya of Ujjain who visited Nepal during the reign of this Amsumantha in B. C. 57, and discredits altogether the part of the Nepala Raja Vamsavali which mentions these events and dates.

In the intoxication of the apparent success he was able to achieve in his nefarious attempt Dr. Buhler has committed himself to several absurd and mutually inconsistent chronological determinations, unaware that he was disprooving his own theory. He has pushed forward the date of the coronation of Sivadeva Varma from B. C. 338 to A. D. 725. He has also fixed the time of the coronation of Amsumantha, the king of the sixth generation after him, which should come off 237 years afterwards ie. according to his own determination of the date of Sivadeva Varma's coronation in A. D., 725, in A. D., 962, strangely in A. D. 637. Is it not absurd and self contradictory ?.

Evidently he resorted to this absurd determination to lend plausibility to the interpolation he had managed to effect, through his friend Dr. Beal, in the Chinese manuscript of the account of Heuntsang's travels and to enhance its value as evidence for the history of Bharat ; and he relied confidently upon the uncritical blind faith of Indian historical scholars, in the veracity and wisdom of the European Orientalists ; for their swallowing the mutual inconsistency in his own statements. As he anticipated, though a century has passed since, our Indian historical scholars continue to repeat his inconsistent statements Parrot-like as though they were sacred texts and to believe implicitly that our own indigenous historical writings are all unreliable without realising or even suspecting the mischief perpetrated by these European Orientalists. It is to render it possible and convenient to attempt such mischief and to distort the truth and reduce the antiquity of the history of Bharat by the concoction of false and baseless theories of their own. That they have been proclaiming incessantly that the accounts of the foreign travellers are more respectable authorities for the reconstruction of our ancient history than the indigenous historical writing and interpolating absurd statements in them to show our indigenous histories to be unreliable. It is clear, with this discussion of the mischief attempted in connection with the history of Nepal, that the alleged writings of Heuntsang, the opinions of Dr. Beal, the history of Nepal by Dr. Buhler and other writings of the European Orientalists are all unreliable. Almost all the chronological determinations in the so-called modern histories of ancient Bharat are wrong and no true history of ancient Bharat can be reconstructed unless we proceed on the basis of the material avilable in our Puranas and start with the Mahabharata War of B. C. 3138 as the foundation for our chronology.

* * * *

## TOPIC - XVI.

### HISTORICITY OF VIKRAMADITYA

The Emperor Vikramaditya was born to Gandharvasena Maharaja in B.C. 101 and belongs to the Panwar dynasty. He was crowned king at Ujjain in B.C. 82 when he was 19 years of age. He reigned for a full century (a hundred years) and passed away at Ujjain in A.D., 19. He conquered the whole of Bharat and reduced all the kings to the status of tributary princes under his suzeraeinty and ruled as Emperor. (His history is given in detail according to the account in the Bhavishya Mahapurana, by this author in chapter VII of his 'Chronology of Ancient Hindu History pt I). It is found recorded in the history of Nepal that he marched with his armies into Nep-.- in B.C., 57, incorporated that kingdom, (the No- thern-most in Bharat) also into his Empire, an- having thus completed his conquest of the whole of Bharat, founded a new Era after him there in Nepal in Kali 3045-44 or B.C. 57. (Vide Indian Antiquary Vol XIII, p. 411 ff).

Even in the history of the kingdom of Magadha there is a detailed account of the kings of the Agni dynasties in the Bhavishya Purana in connection with the four royal dynasties of Pramara, Chayahani, or Tomara, Sukla or Chalukya, Pratihara or Parihara, that ruled over the country after the kings of the Gupta dyanasty.

It is further stated there that the eighth king of the Pramara dynasty, Vikramaditya conquerd the Gupta kingdom of Magadha also and became tho Emperor of Bharat. But the European Orientalists have ignored this portion of the text and denied any place to the kings of all the Agni dynasties in their histories of Bharat.

Thereafter, the 11th king of the same dynasty Salivahana defeated the Sakas, the foreign invaders and founded another Era after his own name in Kali 3179 or A. D., 78 according to the Bhavishya Purana. The 21st king of the same Pramara dyansty is king Bhoja of the glorious literary tradition. In the battle which took place in A. D., 1193 between Prithviraj, of the Tomara dynasty, king of Delhi and Mahammad Ghori, tho king of all these four Agni dynasties (known otherwise as Brahma-Kshatras) took part in the fight to preserve the freedom of the country and lost their lives. The history of all these kings of all these dynasties has been suppressed. There is ample evidence of the historicity of Emporor Vikramaditya in the indigenous histories of Magadha, in Jyotirvidabharana, in Jyotisha Phala Ratnamala, in the Bhashya of (or commentary) the Satapatha Brahmana. (Vide the Authors "Chronology of Kashmir History Reconstructed, from 173 to 222 Pages Ed. 1956.) The writinge of the European Orientalists who indulge in the propaganda that this famous Emperor of India of illustrious tradition was only a fictitious personage, that his equally famous descendent, who also became an Emperor and founded his own Era, Salivahana was also a fictitious personage, are all false propagandist histories.

Our Indian Astronomers prepare their Almanacs (Native Annual Calendars) from year to year reckoning from the Commencement of Kali Yuga till to this date. These Almanacs are in use throughout the country in all all the States. All the Hindus specify this time according to the Kali Saka when they begin the traditional rites prescribed for them.

A. D., 1959 English Calendar year will be 5060 Kaliyuga and 2015-16 Vikrama Saka and 1881 Salivahana Saka.

If from Kali Saka, the Vikrama Saka 2016 years deducted, we get (5060 — 2016) = 3044 Kali Saka or 57 B. C., which will be the starting point of Vikrama Saka. Similarly if we deduct 1881 years of Salivahana Saka from Kali Saka 5060 we get (5060 — 1881) = 3179 Kali Saka or A. D. 78 which will be the starting point of Salivahana Saka.

This proof is enough to show that they are not fictitious personages.

In "Siddhanta Siromani" (Kalamanadhyaya, 28 verse) written by himself Bhaskaracharya, while discussing the calculation of time prevelent during his period spoke about Vikrama and Kali Saka as given below.

"नंदाद्रींदुगुणाश्च (३१७९) विक्रमनृपस्यांते कलेर्वत्सरा:"

This means "That 3179 years in Kaliyuga will be the end of Vikrama Saka".

The beginning of Vikrama Saka will be Kali 3044 years or 57 B. C., and the end of Vikrma Era will be the beginning of Salivahana Saka. When a new Era begins the previous Era is considered to come to a close. So 3179 Kali will be 78 A. D., and this is the beginning of Salivahana Saka. If we deduct from Kali 3179 the Vikrama Saka 3044, we get a period of 135 years. Therefore, this calculation, beyond doubt, confirms the truth of the existence of Vikramaditya in 57 B. C., and the starting of his Era, together with the living of Salivahana in 78 A. D., and the establishing of his Saka. Salivahana was the great Grand son of Vikramarka. So it is evident that Vikramaditya was born in Kali 3001 year or 101 B. C., his Coronation took place in Kali 3020 year or 82 B. C., and the Vikrama Saka was founded in 3044 Kali or 57 B. C. He got dedications of works in Kali 3068 (33 B. C.,) and in Kali 3114 (13 A. D.) from Kalidasa and others. He made Matrugupta, king of Kashmir in Kali 3115 year or 14 A. D., Vikramaditya went to heaven in Kali 3120 year or 19 A. D.

Indisputable statements which prove the authenticity and Historicity of Emperor Vikramaditya will be publihed shortly.

* * * *

# AGE OF THE MAHABHARATA WAR

## TOPIC - XVII.

### SIR WILLIAM JONES,

### PROF. MAX – MULLER AND MR. TROYER

It was Sir William Jones that first laid the foundations in A. D., 1774 for the Modern (false) history of ancient Bharat. He had travelled in central Asia and there secured possession of a document known as the 'Dabistan Paper' in Bactria, containing a list of the kings of the Royal Dynasties of Bactria. They are all Hindu kings. The document shows that previous to the conquests of Alexander in 327 B. C., 153 kings of the dynasty had ruled over Bactria for over 6000 years. So it turned out that the history of the culture and civilisation of Bharat has been in existence for over 6000 years before Alexander and for 2100 years after Alexander up to the time of Sir William Jones, altogether for 8100 years. The discovery really filled him with astonishment.

Thereafter he proposed to reconstruct the history of Ancient Bharat and for that purpose proceeded to Calcutta and there met Pandit Radhakant and asked for information regarding dynastic lists of kings of Bharat if any such were available in our Puranas. The Pandit gave him the lists of the Royal dynasties in the Srimad-bhagavata. Jones took them down in writing and published the same. (Vide Jone's Works, Vol. IV On the Chronology of the Hindus).

Pandit Radhakanta started with the time of the Mahabharata War in B. C. 3138 and gave the lists of kings of the Royal dynasties of Magadha from that time. The first dynasty that ruled in Magadha after the Mahabharata War was the Barhadradha dynasty. The kings of the dynasty numbered 22. They ruled in all for a thousand years. Then the Pradyota dynasty was the next to occupy the throne. The five kings of this dynasty ruled for 138 years in all, the third was the Sisunaga dynasty (10) kings which remained in power for 360 years, the fourth was the Nanda dynasty (9 kings as two generations) which held power only for 100 years. Then as the fifth dynasty the Mauryas seized the throne and came into power. All this information Sir William Jones gathered from the Bhagavata. In the same manner he learned, noted and published that the sixth, the Sunga dynasty, the seventh the Kaanva and the eighth the Andhra dynasty ruled in Magadha in succession and the last king of the Andhra dynasty was Chandrabija or Chandra Sri. He died in B. C. 452. Thus far he could proceed with the information available in the Bhagavata. The succeeding royal dynasties were not available to him with Bhagavata. It did not occur to him that he might refer to the other Puranas. After the close of the rule of the Andhra dynasty, Alexander invaded India in B. C., 326.

This was the history of ancient Bharat which he could learn. He learnt from Pandit Radhakant and recorded in his history the details of the periods of the several kings and of the different royal dynasties beginning with the advent of Kali in B. C. 3102. But he could not relish the fact of such great antiquity of the history of Bharat, refused to recognise the historical truth of the Barhadradha dynasty, alleging that it was perhaps concocted by the Brahmins to increase the antiquity of the history of their country, rejected the 22 kings of the Barhadradha dynasty and their period of 1000 years occupied by their reigns and began his history of Bharat with the pradyota dynasty of about B. C. 2000.

He could see no other way then of reducing the antiquity of the history of Bharat. He Writes:- "On the whole we may safely close the most authentic system of Hindu chronology, that I have been able to procure, with the death of Chandrabija. Should any further information be attainable, we shall, perhaps, in due time attain it either from books or inscriptions in the Sanskrit language, but from the materials with which we are at present supplied, we may establish as indubitable the two following propositions; that the first ages of the Hindus are chiefly mythological, whether their mythology was founded on the dark enigmas of their Astronomers, or on the heroic fictions of their poets and that the fourth, or historical age cannot be carreid further back that about two thousand years before Christ; "(Vide, Jones works, Vol. IV, pp. 42 to 46; 1 and 2 and p. 47, 52).

Subsequently, after consultations with the then Governor General of India Warren Hastings, he gradually veered round to the view that it was not plausible to reject the entire Barhadradha dynasty of Magadha, and it was more plausible to identify wrongly the contemporary in Magadha, of Alexander the Great as Maurya Chandragupta instead of Gupta Chandragupta who they knew was the real contemporary of Alexander and thus reduce the Chronology of the history of Magadha by 1200 years. Ever since, he and other Orientalists of his school of thought, had been suggesting it in their essays contributed to the Asiatic Researches and other journals. After such shy but persistent propaganda in the journals for nearly eighty years, by Jones and his followers, it was Max - Muller who took it up and gave a definite shape and the stamp of his authority to the theory.

## PROF. MAX — MULLER

Prof. Max - Muller had supported the theory of the Central Asian Origin of the Aryans and the theory that they had migrated from Central Asia and invaded India. Lateron, after attempting a translation of the Rig-Veda into his own language, and thus gaining first-hand knowledge, to some extent, of the literature of Bharat, he renounced his Central Asian theory and came round to the view that the Aryans were the native inhabitants of the region round the

Ganges, the Europeans were all descended from them, and it was the birth place of the entire human race.

"What have we inharited from the dark dwellers on the Indus and the Ganges ? Their historical records extend in some respects, so far beyond all other records and have been preserved to us in such perfect and such legible documents, than we can learn from them lessons which we can learn nowhere else."

"What then is it that gives to Sanskrit its claim on our attention and its supreme importance in the eyes of the historians ? First of all its antiquity for we know Sanskrit at an earlier period than the Greek. But what is far more important than its mere chronological antiquity in the antiquie state of preservation, in which that Aryan language has been handed down to us."

Again he says :- "As Sankrit stepped into the midst of these languages (Viz. Greek, Latin, Gothic Anglo-saxon, Celtic, Slavonic etc.,) there came light and warmth and mutual recognition. They all ceased to be strangers and each fell of its own accord into its right place. Sanskrit was the eldest sister of them all and could tell of many things which the other members of the family had quite forgotten."

"All I wish to impress on you by way of introduction that, the result of science of language, which without the aid of Sanskrit, would never have been obtained, from the essential elements of we call a liberal, that is, a historical education— an education which will enable a man to do what the French call S, Orienter, that is, 'to find his East', 'his true East', and thus to determine his real place in the world".

"We all come from the East—all that we value most has come to us from the East" (Max-Muller's, "India What can it teach us" pp. 21 to 32 Ed. 1883).

"To fathom ancient India, all knowledge acquired in Europe avails naught, the study must recommence as the infant learns to read, and the harvest is too distant for lukewarm energies".

"Then you will have been initiated, and India, will apper to you the mother of human race— the cradle of all our traditions. The Hindu emigration rendered the same service to Egypt, to Persia, Judia, Greece and Rome is What I suppose to demonstrate." (Ibid. p. 17)

Max - Muller has professed great respect for the culture and wisdom of Bharat. He is well-known as an admirer and friend of Bharat. Such a respectable Scholar was induced by presure brought to bear on him by the Orientalists, to exprses it as his opinion in A. D., 1859 that Chandragupta of the Maurya dynasty was the contemporary in India of Alexander the Great, and thus to fix the foundations for their false history of ancient Bharat. Till then the European Orientalists were basing their historical writings and chronological determinations relating to the history of ancient Bharat on the contemporaneity of Alexander and Chandragupta Maurya as sugges--ted in the articles in the journals but thereafter they were openly assuming the suggested theory as a proved fact on the strength of the declara--tion by Max-Muller in his history of Sanskrit Literature. But Max-Muller has expressed his opinion, carefully without keeping back the circumastances and motives with which he was obli-ged to make the declaration, so that it is possible for Indian historians, if only they care, to detect the mischief and remedy it even from the wording of his own declaration. He says "The history of India can be connected with that of Greece and its chronology be reduced to its proper limits,........". (Vide History of Ancient Sanskrit Literature by Prof. Max - Muller 1859 Edn., Pages 3-8 and Allahabad Edn. pp. 141-143). Perhaps Max - Muller hoped that Indian historical scholars would in course of time discover, the motive of the identification rectify the deliberation reduction of the antiquity of their ancient history and hinted at it indirectly. But our historical scholars have not taken the hint so far.

## MR. M. TROYER

He had translated the text of Kalhana's Rajatarangini into English. He published his objection to the declaration by Max - Muller supporting the theory of the contemporaneity of Alexander and Maurya Chandragupta. He declared that the contemporary of Alexander was not Chandragupta of the Mourya dynasty but only Chandragupta of the Gupta dynasty of Magadha and sent his opinion in writing to prof. Max-Muller. Othermen of integrity among the European Orientalists, had also written to prof. Max-Muller pointing out his error. But since he had knowingly through pressure brought to bear on him, expressed his erroneous opinion. So he did not withdraw his opinion, but unable to advance any proof or authority in support of his view, wrote :- "Although other scholars and particularly Mr. Troyer in his edition of the Rajatarangini, have raised objections, we shall see that the evidence in favour of identity of Chandragupta and Sandrocyptus is such as to admit of no reasonable doubt (Vide History of Ancient Sanskrit Literature pp, 3-8 of 1859 Edn. p4, 243 of Allahabad Edn.,).

Stamped with the authority of the great scholar, Max - Muller, this false theory has been working havoc with the history of ancient Bharat. It has been responsible for casting doubts on every historical event in the history of Bharat. Since it is contrary to the entire literature of Bharat it has corrupted the entire history of ancient Bharat. The difference between the time of Maurya Chandragupta 1534 B. C. and Gupta Chndragupta B. C. 327 is nearly 1207 years. The time of the Mahabarata war of

B. C. 3138 is pushed forward thereby to B. C. 1931. With regard to every important Chronological determination the difference between the erroneous determination of the European Orientalists and the true determination according to the historical writings in indigenous literature of the country turns out to be just about 1200 years.

Max - Muller was not able to show any authority or argument against the objections of Mr. Troyer and others of his way of thought. The authority of the writings of the Chinese traveller, discovered and manipulated later, was not available to him at that time, perhaps the note of repentence for the mischief with which he had corporated is evident in these words of the proffessor :- "No nation has in this respect been more unjustly treated than the Indian. Not only have general conclusions been drawn from the most scanty materials but the most questionable and spurious authorities have been employed without the least historical investigation." (Quoted from Max - Muller's writings by Mr. Krishnamachariar in his 'History of Classical Sanskrit Literature,' Introduction pp. LXXXIV and LXXXV).

* * * *

# AGE OF THE MAHABHARATA WAR

## TOPIC - XVIII.

### TRUE CHRONOLOGY OF ANCIENT HISTORY OF BHARAT

There is an account of the Chronology according to the Kaliyuga Raja Vrittanta, a Purana in which all the information available in all the Puranas has been collated and reconciled. For details refer to this author's "Ancient Hindu History Pt. I.".

1. The time of the Mahabharata War - 36 years before Kali which commenced in B. C. 3102.

| | No. of kings reigned | No. of year reigned |
|---|---|---|
| 1. The Barhadradha dynasty .... .... | 22 kings. | 1006 years. |
| 2. The Pradyota dynasty .... .... | 5 „ | 138 „ |
| 3. The Sisunaga dynasty .... .... | 10 „ | 360 „ |
| 4. The Nanda dynasty .... .... | 2 „ | 100 „ |
| 5. The Maurya dynasty .... .... | 12 „ | 316 „ |
| 6. The Sunga dynasty .... .... | 10 „ | 300 „ |
| 7. Kanwa dynasty .... | 4 „ | 85 „ |
| 8. The Andhra dynasty .... .... | 32 „ | 506 „ |
| | 97 | 2811 years. |

| | | | |
|---|---|---|---|
| B. F. .... | 97 | 2811 years | |
| From the Mahabharata War to the end of the Andhra dynasty 3138 — 2811 = 327 B. C.... | | | till 327 B. C. |
| 9. Andhra Bhritya or Gupta dynasty .... | 7 | 245 | 82 „ |
| 10. Panwar dynasty. No. 8 of this dynasty is Emperor Vikrama who founded the Vikrama Era -- his dynasty. .... | 24 | 1275 | 1193 A. D. |
| | 128 | 4331 | 1193 A. D. |

In the year 1193 A. D. all the four princes of the four Agni Dynasties, fighting on the side of Prithwiraj against Md. Ghori, king of Delhi who was one of them, and a prince of the Tomara dynasty, died on the battle field a death always coveted by heroes in this land of Bharat. They died an honourable death fighting in defence of the independence of their country.

2. From The time of the Mahabharata War of B. C. 3138 down to end of the Andhra Dynasty of Magadha 327 B. C. .... .... 2811 years
Kings of the Gupta dynasty .... 245 years
Kings of the Panwar dynasty .... 1275 years

Total 4331 years

For a total period of 4331 years Hindu kings had reigned as Emperors over the whole of Bharat

| | | |
|---|---|---|
| from Mahabharata War .... .... | 3138 | B. C. |
| Battle of Thaneswar .... .... | 1193 | A. D. |
| Total | 4331 | years. |

3. The reckoning in the Puranas based on the movement of the Constellation of the Seven Sages

| | | |
|---|---|---|
| From the time of the Mahabharata War when the Seven Sages were in Magha to the time of Mahapadma Nanda .... | 1504 | years. |
| Mahapadma Nanda to the time of the Andhras- when they pass into the 24th star after Magha .... .... | 801 | ,, |
| | 2305 | ,, |
| The period of the rule of the Andhra Dynasty .... | 506 | |
| To the end of the Andhra dynasty or the beginning of the Gupta dynasty. | 2811 | ,, |

| | | |
|---|---|---|
| 4. From the time of the Mahabharata War by the time of the end of the reign of the 24th king of the Andhra dynasty the Seven Sages complete a full cycle of 27 stars and reach Magha again. .... | 2705 | years |

| | | |
|---|---|---|
| B. F. | .... | 2705 years |
| The period of the rule of the remaining kings of the Andhra dynasty from the 25th king .... .... | .... | 106 „ |
| From the Mahabharata War to the end of the Andhra dynasty .... | .... | 2811 years |
| Then the period of the reigns of the Guptas | | 245 „ |
| Panwar Dynasty or Brahma Kahatra Dynasty .... | .... | 1275 „ |
| | | 4331 years. |

The total period of the rule of 128 Hindu kings from the time of the Mahabharata War is 4331 years. Average length of the reign of each king is 34 years.

The Mahabharata, the Puranas, the Astronomical treatises of the country, the Native Calendars tradition and indigenous historical writings like the histories of Magadha, Kashmir and Nepal the entire ancient literature of Bharat, unanimously declare the time of the Mahabharata War to be 36 years before Kali or 3138 B. C.

| | |
|---|---|
| From the year of the Mahabharata War or the year 1 of the Yudhishtira Era, the period of the rule of the Hindu kings. | 4331 years |

| | |
|---|---|
| B. F. .... .... | 4331 years |
| The later period during which the Muhammadan, the Maharashtras and Siks and the English ruled over the country ie. from A. D. 1193 – 1947 when India attained Independence. | 753 ,, |
| Since the attainment of Independence on 15th August 1947 up to 1959 A. D. .... .... | 12 ,, |
| | 5096 years |

5096 Yudhishtira Era=5060 Kali Era=1959A.D.
SO, THE TIME OF THE MAHABHARATA WAR IS KALI 5096 – 1959 A. D. = 3138 B. C.

* —— *

## CONCLUSION

From what has been stated in Mahabharat-Puranas, Atronomical books, Inscriptions, history of Magadha as detailed in Puranas now styled as Indian History, Kashmir and Nepal histories, movement of Saptarshimandala, the periods over which different dynasties of kings ruled as described in Puranas, history of Vikramaditya and Ancient Hindu History, it has been proved that the Mahabharata War was 3138 B. C. This has also been confirmed by the evidence obtained from inscriptions. Amongst these inscriptions, the Aihole inscription put up by Pualakesin the second in 634 A. D., has been universally accepted as Gospel truth by all historians. This inscription clearly points out without any ambiguity that the Bharata War was is 3138 B. C. It is therefore confirmed beyond doubt by all the above mentioned proofs that the Mahabharata War was is 3138 B. C.

I Therfore, appeal to our Indian historians to study the texts of our indigenous historical writings in the originals, ascertain truth, reject the false and fantastic histories of Ancient Bharat concocted by the European Orientalists and attempt a reconstruction of the true history of Ancient Bharat.

JAI BHARAT